T0114881

Books and Writings by Jim Zeigler

Books:

*Look Up: Redemption
in this Generation
2016*

*Look Out: The World
Without Christians
2018*

*Look Around: God's
New World Order
2020*

*He Sent His Son
2017*

*It's in the Book
2019*

Other Writings on Website: jimzeiglerbooks.com

Mommy - I Love Your, Hey Dad,
America - Prepare to meet thy God,
The Last Blood, The Visit, In the Gap,
Passover Passion. The Real Innkeeper.

Look Around

God's New World Order

A Look at the Future Book Three

Jim Zeigler

WESTBOW
PRESS®
A DIVISION OF THOMAS NELSON
& ZONDERVAN

WestBow Press books may be ordered through booksellers or by contacting:

WestBow Press
A Division of Thomas Nelson & Zondervan
1663 Liberty Drive
Bloomington, IN 47403
www.westbowpress.com
844-714-3454

Scripture taken from the King James Version of the Bible.

ISBN: 978-1-6642-0449-2 (sc)
ISBN: 978-1-6642-0448-5 (e)

Print information available on the last page.

WestBow Press rev. date: 10/05/2020

To Carol, my wife of fifty-five years.
You have been my inspiration and encouragement. You have
withstood Satan's attacks and have been my faithful prayer warrior.
Thank you, and I Love you.

Contents

Introduction

There are four chapters in the Bible where Satan's influence is not seen. These are Genesis one and two, which occur before the sinful fall of man and Revelation twenty-one and twenty-two, that describes the glories of the Millennial Kingdom and Heaven after God casts Satan into the Lake of Fire.

Jesus is the First and the Last, the Beginning and the End, and thus knows the complete world history, past, present, and future time ends.

Since the time of creation, Satan has been in a constant battle against God to overthrow His control of the Earth and humanity. This battle will not end until Satan is defeated, judged, and being punished in the Lake of the Fire for eternity. In the meantime, he battles to gain control of God's creation and place himself as the God of this world. He will succeed and rule the world for a short seven-year period of hell on earth before Yeshua; the Messiah sentences him to the Lake of Fire.

I began a series of three books in 2016 to inform those living in the End Times of what to expect as God brings rescue to His saints and judgment to His enemies.

In my first book, about the End Times titled **"Lookup: Redemption in this Generation,"** I tried to explain the world situation at the time when Christ will return for the Church. Commonly called the Rapture.

The second writing, **"Look Out: The World without Christians,"** deals with the preparation for and the events of the seven years when God brings judgment to the unbelieving on Earth, ending Satan's rule and reclaiming the world Adam gave to Satan when he rebelled against God.

This third book titled **"Look Around: God's New World Order"** is about life in the Millennium, the one-thousand-year reign of Christ on earth, and also our eternal home in Heaven.

Now, as we close this period of human history, we need to know what God has planned for the near and distant future. If you believe that Jesus died for your sins and reconciled you with Jehovah God, then you should look for the Rapture of the Church and Jesus' glorious return to take us to be with Him.

> *"Let not your heart be troubled: ye believe in God, believe also in me. In my Father's house are many mansions: if it were not so, I would have told you. I go to prepare a place for you. And if I go and prepare a place for you, I will come again, and receive you unto myself; that where I am, there ye may be also." John 14:1-3.*

If you don't believe this, then it's time to prepare for the terrible time ahead for those who dwell on the Earth. The seven years of God's judgment is about to fall. So now you need to either **Look Up** or **Look Out**.

The Dispensations of the Earth:

"New Testament thoughts are derived from traditional Judaism and understand that the first 6,000 years is known as the present age/world (Olam Hazeh). These first 6,000 years are divided into three distinct 2,000-year periods of time or ages:

The first 2,000 years from the creation of Adam to the time of Abraham is known as the period/age of innocence where no Written Torah existed, and all Torah were passed down from generation to generation, thus the Oral Torah.

*The next two thousand years from the time of Abraham to the expected arrival of the Jewish Moshiach ben Yosef (**Jesus son of Joseph**) is known as the period/age of the Letter of the Torah. Meaning if you willfully break the Instructions, and it is observed by two witnesses, you die.*

The final 2,000 years of time within the 6,000 years of the present/age world is known as the days of the Messiah (Yemot Mashiach), as from when Moshiach came to correctly explain the Torah and is classified as Under the Grace of the Torah. Meaning that Moshiach paid the death penalty for His adherents who are now under His grace, but still adhering to Torah. There is no physical governmental death penalty now for violating Torah, but continuing to break Torah willfully will result is spiritual death (Heb 10:26).

*The last 1,000 years is known as the Messianic Era or the future age/coming where the Temple will be rebuilt, and each Instruction of the Torah will be in full effect again. This is when Moshiach will rule the world with a rod of iron (Rev 2:27, 12:5, 19:15). Thus the 7,000-year plan of Ha-Shem (**the Name**) is a major concept and foundational truth in understanding Bible prophecy and eschatology.* Prof. (Dr.) WA. Liebenberg.

If you know the Lord as your Saviour, then you can look for 1,000 years of peace on Earth in which God will remake the Earth to be like Eden. Then after God judges those born in the Millenium and passes judgment on all sinners of all ages at the Great White Throne judgment, you can spend eternity **Look**ing **Around** the new Heaven and New Earth. (Rev 21:1).

> *"And I saw a new heaven and a new earth: for the first heaven and the first earth were passed away; and there was no more sea." Revelation 21:1.*

Part One

The Thousand-Year
Reign of Christ

1

Campaign of Armageddon

"And I saw an angel come down from heaven, having the key of the bottomless pit and a great chain in his hand. And he laid hold on the dragon, that old serpent, which is the Devil, and Satan, and bound him a thousand years, And cast him into the bottomless pit, and shut him up, and set a seal upon him, that he should deceive the nations no more, till the thousand years should be fulfilled: and after that, he must be loosed a little season." Revelation 20:1-3.

Jesus rode into Jerusalem on Sunday the 10th of the Hebrew Nissan 32AD and was hailed as the King of the Jews. For the next three days, He taught in the Temple and was challenged by the Pharisees and Scribes, proving He was the Son of God. Matthew records His woes on the Scribes and the Pharisees, calling them Hypocrites. Then He tells *'the multitude and his disciples,...*

Behold, your house is left unto you, desolate. For I say unto you, Ye shall not see me henceforth, till ye shall say, Blessed, is he that cometh in the name of the Lord.' And the next day, the same crowd was shouting, **"Crucify him, crucify him."** The following Sunday, He rose from the dead and ascended into heaven, promising to return when Israel repented and prayed for his return.

After Two Days Days

Before the Lord returns at His Second Coming, Israel must first confess the nation's sin and, second, plead for the Messiah's return.

> *"I will go and return to my place, till they acknowledge their offense, and seek my face: in their affliction, they will seek me early. Come, and let us return unto the LORD: for he hath torn, and he will heal us; he hath smitten, and he will bind us up. After two days will he revive us: in the third day he will raise us up, and we shall live in his sight. Then shall we know, if we follow on to know the LORD: his going forth is prepared as the morning; and he shall come unto us as the rain, as the latter and former rain unto the earth." Hosea 5:15-6:1-3.*

This passage tells us that Messiah will return after two days. Psalm 90:4 informs us that to God, *"a thousand years in thy sight are but as yesterday when it is past, and as a watch in the night."* Jesus came the first time as a sacrifice for sin; He would come again in two days of about two thousand years. Two thousand years have passed since Jesus rode into Jerusalem as the Servant on a donkey. When He enters Jerusalem, this time, He will come as a conquering

King on a white charger. The New Testament speaks of the same time interval in Peter's second letter.

> *"But, beloved, be not ignorant of this one thing, that one day is with the Lord as a thousand years, and a thousand years as one day." 2 Peter 3:8*

However, only after Israel repents and confesses her national sins can the physical blessings that Israel once enjoyed be restored to her. The leaders of Israel will finally recognize the reason the Tribulation has fallen on them. Probably a result of the study of the ancient scriptures, the preaching of the 144,000 Jewish Missionaries, the testimonies of the two witnesses, and literature left behind by the church saints. The national regeneration will come through a national confession. Isaiah foretells the coming of Jesus as the Messiah and Saviour and his crucifixion:

> *"Who hath believed our report? And to whom is the arm of the LORD revealed? For he shall grow up before him as a tender plant, and as a root out of a dry ground: he hath no form nor comeliness; and when we shall see him, there is no beauty that we should desire him. He is despised and rejected of men; a man of sorrows and acquainted with grief: and we hid as it were our faces from him; he was despised, and we esteemed him not. Surely he hath borne our griefs, and carried our sorrows: yet we did esteem him stricken, smitten of God, and afflicted. But he was wounded for our transgressions; he was bruised for our iniquities: the chastisement of our peace was upon him, and with his stripes, we are healed. All we like sheep have gone astray; we have turned every one to his own way, and the*

LORD hath laid on him the iniquity of us all. He was oppressed, and he was afflicted, yet he opened not his mouth: he is brought as a lamb to the slaughter, and as a sheep, before her shearers is dumb, so he openeth not his mouth. He was taken from prison and from judgment: and who shall declare his generation? For he was cut off out of the land of the living: for the transgression of my people was he stricken. And he made his grave with the wicked, and with the rich in his death; because he had done no violence, neither was any deceit in his mouth. Isaiah 53:1-9.

Jesus entered the Temple in Jerusalem, hailed as King on the day we now call Palm Sunday, and was rejected by national Israel four days later. Matthew records the result of his rejection.

"Behold, your house [Temple] is left unto you desolate [without the glory of God]. For I say unto you, Ye shall not see me henceforth, till ye shall say, Blessed, is he that cometh in the name of the Lord." Matthew 26:38-39.

This public confession must fulfill the prophecy of the Apostle Paul so that the nation of *"Israel shall be saved."*

"For I would not, brethren, that ye should be ignorant of this mystery, lest ye should be wise in your own conceits; that blindness in part is happened to Israel until the fulness of the Gentiles be come in. And so all Israel shall be saved: as it is written, There shall come out of Sion the Deliverer, and shall turn away ungodliness from

Jacob: For this is my covenant unto them when I shall take away their sins." Romans 11:25-27.

"Jesus will return at the request of Israel and enter battle with the Antichrist and his armies. With his return to the remnant of Israel and Bozrah, he will indeed save the tents of Judah first, before saving the Jews of Jerusalem as Zachariah 12:7 predicted:" Arnold Fruchtenbaum.

"The LORD also shall save the tents of Judah first, that the glory of the house of David and the glory of the inhabitants of Jerusalem do not magnify themselves against Judah." Zechariah 12:7

Since Jesus will save the **tents of Judah** first, meaning those in temporary dwelling places shows that the initial site of His return is Bozrah and not the Mount of Olives.

While the battle between Messiah and the Antichrist will begin in Bozrah, it will continue all the way back to the eastern walls of Jerusalem, which overlooked a section of the Kidron Valley, also known as the valley of Jehoshaphat. The prophet Joel records it this way:

"Let the heathen be wakened, and come up to the valley of Jehoshaphat: for there will I sit to judge all the heathen roundabout. Put ye in the sickle, for the harvest is ripe: come, get you down; for the press is full, the vats overflow; for their wickedness is great." Joel 3:12-13.

Among the first casualties will be the Antichrist himself.

"And then shall that Wicked be revealed, whom the Lord shall consume with the spirit of his mouth, and shall destroy with the brightness of his coming." 2 Thessalonians 2:8.

The one who claimed to be God and performed all kinds of miracles, signs, and wonders, the one to exercise the authority of Satan and ruled the world, will be quickly dispensed by the Word of Jesus, the Messiah.

The Valley of Blood:

After the death of the Antichrist, the slaughter of his army will continue. The Bible describes the Messiah marching through the land in indignation and treading the nations with His feet and cutting them down with His words, causing blood to be sprinkled on his garments as we see in Zachariah 12. The fight continues to Jerusalem, ending in the Valley of Jehoshaphat. The king of the Jews will tread the armies that gathered against the Jews. This is what John speaks of in Revelation Fourteen.

> *"And the angel thrust in his sickle into the earth, and gathered the vine of the earth, and cast it into the great winepress of the wrath of God. And the winepress was trodden without the city, and blood came out of the winepress, even unto the horse bridles, by the space of a thousand and six hundred furlongs." Revelation 14:19-20.*

Because of this final battle, the blood stretches for 1600 furlongs, which is approximately 200 miles. The 200 miles may cover the entire area from the valley of Armageddon to Bozrah, or it may refer to the valley from Jerusalem to the Red Sea. The battle will end in the Valley of Jehoshaphat.

After the actual fighting is completed and Jesus ends the battles, He will make the victory ascent up the Mount of Olives as described by Zachariah:

"Then shall the LORD go forth, and fight against those nations, as when he fought in the day of battle. And his feet shall stand in that day upon the Mount of Olives, which is before Jerusalem on the east..." Zechariah 14:3-4a.

"In Zechariah 14, Jehovah is seen as coming forth to fight against the nations that have gathered against the Jews (v3). It is only after the fighting of verse three that his feet will stand upon the Mount of Olives," Dr. Arnold Fruchtenbaum.

As the victory assent upon the Mount of Olives occurs, several cataclysmic events bring the Great Tribulation to an end. With the seventh bowl judgment, a voice cries out, *"it is done."*

"And the seventh angel poured out his vial into the air; and there came an influential voice out of the temple of heaven, from the throne, saying, It is done." Revelation 16:17.

At the conclusion of the Battle of Armageddon, the seventh angel will release the seventh bowl, containing the judgment of a world-shaking earthquake. This last earthquake will devastate the entire planet. God will divide Jerusalem into three parts, and the cities of the nations will crumble. Every island will move away, and the mountains will crumble. Great hailstones that the Bible says will weigh a talent (over 100 pounds) will also accompany these terrible judgments.

Besides the city of Jerusalem dividing into three parts, the Mount of Olives will divide into two parts, creating a valley running east to west and providing an escape route for the Jewish inhabitants of Jerusalem. The inhabitants of Jerusalem will be rescued following the deliverance of the other Jews in Bozrah.

> *"And his feet shall stand in that day upon the Mount of Olives, which is before Jerusalem on the east, and the mount of Olives shall cleave in the midst thereof toward the east and toward the west, and there shall be a very great valley; and half of the mountain shall remove toward the north and half of it toward the south. And ye shall flee to the valley of the mountains; for the valley of the mountains shall reach unto Azal: yea, ye shall flee, like as ye fled from before the earthquake in the days of Uzziah king of Judah: and the LORD my God shall come, and all the saints with thee." Zechariah 14:4-5.*

Jesus told his disciples on the same mountain that when he returns, there would also be a worldwide blackout.

> *"Immediately after the tribulation of those days shall the sun be darkened, and the moon shall not give her light, and the stars shall fall from heaven, and the powers of the heavens shall be shaken: And then shall appear the sign of the Son of man in heaven: and then shall all the tribes of the earth mourn, and they shall see the Son of man coming in the clouds of heaven with power and great glory. And he shall send his angels with a great sound of a trumpet, and they shall gather together his elect from the four winds, from one end of heaven to the other." Matthew 24:29-31.*

The prophet Joel foretold of the earthquake and the blackout that occurs at the end of the Day of Jehovah:

"Multitudes, multitudes in the valley of decision: for the day of the LORD is near in the valley of decision. The sun and the moon shall be darkened, and the stars shall withdraw their shining. The LORD also shall roar out of Zion, and utter his voice from Jerusalem, and the heavens and the earth shall shake: but the LORD will be the hope of his people, and the strength of the children of Israel. So shall ye know that I am the LORD your God dwelling in Zion, my holy mountain: then shall Jerusalem be holy, and there shall no strangers pass through her any more." Joel 3:14-17.

The pleading of Israel for the Messiah to return will not be confined to the Jews in Basra but will include the Jews still in Jerusalem. It will begin with a confession of their national sins, followed by a plea for Messiah Jesus to return and save them from the troubles surrounding them. During Israel's mourning, they will call to the One whom they have pierced for the outpouring of the Holy Spirit and the cleansing of their land. After Israel's plea for Messiah to come, he will return to Earth, not to the Mount of Olives as is commonly taught, but to a place known as Basra.

"Come near, ye nations, to hear; and hearken, ye people: let the earth hear, and all that is therein; the world, and all things that come forth of it. For the indignation of the LORD is upon all nations, and his fury upon all their armies: he hath utterly destroyed them, he hath delivered them to the slaughter. Their slain also shall be cast out, and their stink shall come up out of their carcasses, and the mountains shall be melted with their blood. And all the host of heaven shall be dissolved, and the heavens shall be rolled

together as a scroll: and all their host shall fall down, as the leaf falleth off from the vine, and as a falling fig from the fig tree. For my sword shall be bathed in heaven: behold, it shall come down upon Idumea, and upon the people of my curse, to judgment. The sword of the LORD is filled with blood, it is made fat with fatness, and with the blood of lambs and goats, with the fat of the kidneys of rams: for the LORD hath a sacrifice in Bozrah, and a great slaughter in the land of Idumea. And the unicorns shall come down with them, and the bullocks with the bulls; and their land shall be soaked with blood, and their dust made fat with fatness." Isaiah 34:1-7.

Isaiah's call is to the nations and to their armies declaring that God has anger against them. He has destined them to be slaughtered by the sword of the Lord. He reports that when the sword of the Lord strikes, it will be in the land of Edom, at the city of Bozrah in Southern Jordan. Isaiah describes the same situation in 63:1-6. Isaiah, the prophet, was standing on a high point or mountain in Israel looking eastward toward the land of Edom when he saw a magnificent but bloodstained figure approaching him in glory and splendor.

"Who is this that cometh from Edom, with dyed garments from Bozrah? this that is glorious in his apparel, traveling in the greatness of his strength? I that speak in righteousness, mighty to save." Isaiah 63:1.

The figure coming to Isaiah from the city of Bozrah, in the land of Edom and having greatness in His strength, arrayed with the Shekinah glory of God, is the Jewish Messiah Himself. Isaiah's question is answered in the rest of the verse. Only one man has the power to answer, *"I that speak in righteousness,"* and that is *"mighty to save."* This is the person of Jesus, the Messiah, marching toward Jerusalem. Isaiah responds with a second question.

"Wherefore art thou red in thine apparel, and thy garments like him that treadeth in the winefat?" Isaiah 63:2.

Isaiah notices that the Messiah's clothing, though glorified with the Shekinah glory, is stained with blood. So Isaiah inquires why Jesus' garments became stained.

"I have trodden the winepress alone; and of the people, there was none with me: for I will tread them in mine anger, and trample them in my fury; and their blood shall be sprinkled upon my garments, and I will stain all my raiment. For the day of vengeance is in mine heart, and the year of my redeemed is come. And I looked, and there was none to help; and I wondered that there was none to uphold: therefore mine own arm brought salvation unto me; and my fury, it upheld me. And I will tread down the people in mine anger, and make them drunk in my fury, and I will bring down their strength to the earth." Isaiah 63:3-6.

The bloodstains were from the battle fought by Jesus, the Messiah in the land of Edom, and the city of Bozrah. In the course of trampling the nations, their lifeblood sprinkled his garments, staining them red. The fight was necessary to save his people, Israel. He fought all alone.

"And out of his mouth goeth a sharp sword, that with it he should smite the nations: and he shall

rule them with a rod of iron: and he treadeth the winepress of the fierceness and wrath of Almighty God." Revelation 19:15

By the time Messiah reaches Jerusalem, His garments are already stained with the blood from the slaughter of His enemies. At the second coming, the Messiah will enter battle with the forces of the Antichrist in Jerusalem.

"And then shall appear the sign of the Son of man in heaven: and then shall all the tribes of the earth mourn, and they shall see the Son of man coming in the clouds of heaven with power and great glory." Matthew 24:30.

Jesus, the Son of Man, will return to Earth in a cloud of Shekinah glory just as He had ascended to heaven. Luke described this event in the book of Acts.

"And when he had spoken these things, while they beheld, he was taken up; and a cloud received him out of their sight. And while they looked stedfastly toward heaven as he went up, behold, two men stood by them in white apparel; Which also said, Ye men of Galilee, why stand ye gazing up into heaven? this same Jesus, which is taken up from you into heaven, shall so come in like manner as ye have seen him go into heaven.: Acts 1:9-11

The two angels told the disciples that Jesus would return in the same way as they saw Him leave. But did not say to the same place from which he had left. The Lord left into the clouds of heaven and will return in the clouds of heaven, the Shekinah glory. The apostle John the Revelator describes His second coming:

"And I saw heaven opened, and behold a white horse, and he that sat upon him was called Faithful and True, and in righteousness, he doth judge and make war. His eyes were as a flame of fire, and on his head were many crowns; and he had a name written, that no man knew, but he himself. And he was clothed with a vesture dipped in blood: and his name is called The Word of God. And the armies which were in heaven followed him upon white horses, clothed in fine linen, white and clean. And out of his mouth goeth a sharp sword, that with it he should smite the nations: and he shall rule them with a rod of iron: and he treadeth the winepress of the fierceness and wrath of Almighty God. And he hath on his vesture and on his thigh a name is written, KING OF KINGS, AND LORD OF LORDS." Revelation 19:11-16.

This passage is describing the Messiah as the judge; He makes war against the nations because he is faithful and true. He wears a crown showing His royalty, and His garments are stained with the blood of His enemies described in Isaiah 63. This is the coming of the judge, the incarnate Word of God, Jesus returning in righteousness to judge the nations.

The Great Tribulation and the Campaign of Armageddon will end with these cataclysmic events. With God's judgment on Satan, the Antichrist, the False Prophet, Christ's reign as Lord of Lords and King of Kings will begin and last for a thousand years.

After the Battle of Armageddon, the seventh angel will pour out the seventh and last bowl judgment, containing a colossal earthquake. This last earthquake will devastate the whole Earth.

2

First Seventy-Five Days

"I beheld the earth, and, lo, it was without form, and void; and the heavens, and they had no light. I beheld the mountains, and, lo, they trembled, and all the hills moved lightly. I beheld, and, lo, there was no man, and all the birds of the heavens were fled. I beheld, and, lo, the fruitful place was a wilderness, and all the cities thereof were broken down at the presence of the LORD, and by his fierce anger. For thus hath the LORD said, The whole land shall be desolate; yet will I not make a full end. For this shall the earth mourn, and the heavens above be black: because I have spoken it, I have purposed it, and will not repent, neither will I turn back from it." Jeremiah 4:23-28.

The world that Jesus Christ will take reign over will be almost uninhabitable. The land structures are collapsed, and skyscrapers are in the streets, the world is full of death, over half the world's population has been killed, the dams in the rivers are destroyed. The oceans are full of dead fish and sea creatures, and the islands are moved or sunk as the tectonic plates shift the continents. The Sun, Moon, and stars of heaven are darkened because of the war against God and the earthquakes, volcanoes, and nuclear explosions.

> *"And I saw an angel come down from heaven, having the key of the bottomless pit and a great chain in his hand. And he laid hold on the dragon, that old serpent, which is the Devil, and Satan, and bound him a thousand years, And cast him into the bottomless pit, and shut him up, and set a seal upon him, that he should deceive the nations no more, till the thousand years should be fulfilled: and after that, he must be loosed a little season." Revelation 20:1-3.*

No more will Satan charge our impulses of lust, anger, fear, and hate as he will be confined for 1000 years. The hallmark of the millennium will be holiness. Our tendencies toward sin and rebellion will be restrained because Jesus is in charge. In this new Satan free world, God's discipline will still be required among the non-glorified citizens of the world to avoid spiritual failure. Even without the inspiration of Satan, they will yet have a sin nature passed down from Adam with the potential for evil within themselves.

From this chaos, the creator, Jesus, will resurrect a new and better world.

> *"In the beginning was the Word, and the Word was with God, and the Word was God. The same was in the beginning with God. All things were*

made by him; and without him was not any thing made that was made." John 1:1-3.

The 1260, 1290, 1335 Days:

The books of Daniel and Revelation are often studied together because their prophecies concerning the end times dovetail with each other nicely. Both books agree that the first half of the Tribulation, from the rise of the Antichrist to his elevating himself as god, is 1260 or three and one-half years. They appear to have different times for the remaining number of days known as the Great Tribulation period: Daniel mentions 1,290 days and 1,335 days; Revelation says 1,260 days, for a total "discrepancy" of 75 days (1,335 minus 1,260 = 75).

> *"From the time that the daily sacrifice is abolished and the abomination that causes desolation is set up, there will be 1,290 days. Blessed is the one who waits for and reaches the end of the 1,335 days." Daniel 12:11–12.*

> *"And I will appoint my two witnesses, and they will prophesy for 1,260 days, clothed in sackcloth." Revelation 11:3.*

"Both of these prophecies deal with specific time periods associated with the seven-year tribulation.

Another verse in Daniel establishes the length of two-time segments in the tribulation: "[The prince who is to come] will confirm a covenant with many for one 'seven.' In the middle of the 'seven' he will put an end to sacrifice and offering. And at the temple, he will set up an abomination that causes desolation, until the end that is decreed is poured out on him' (Daniel 9:27). The "prince who is to come,' is the Antichrist or the "beast,' of Revelation.

According to Daniel 9:27, the tribulation begins with the signing of a peace treaty between the Antichrist and Israel, intended to be for one "seven," that is, a set of seven years. But the "seven" is divided into halves: midway through the seven years, the Antichrist breaks the treaty and sets up a sacrilegious object in the Temple (the "abomination that causes desolation"). The phrase "in the middle" indicates that the first half of the tribulation lasts for 3½ years (1,260 days, using a "prophetic year" of 360 days). Likewise, the second half of the tribulation lasts another 1,260 days (another 3½ years), for a total of seven years. Revelation 11:3 "specifically mentions 1,260 days, which corresponds exactly with Daniel's prophecy of the abomination of desolation," www. got questions.org.

"And I heard, but I understood not: then said I, O my Lord, what shall be the end of these things? And he said, Go thy way, Daniel: for the words are closed up and sealed till the time of the end. Many shall be purified, and made white, and tried; but the wicked shall do wickedly: and none of the wicked shall understand; but the wise shall understand. And from the time that the daily sacrifice shall be taken away, and the abomination that maketh desolate set up, there shall be a thousand two hundred and ninety days. Blessed is he that waiteth and cometh to the thousand three hundred and five and thirty days. But go thou thy way till the end be: for thou shalt rest and stand in thy lot at the end of the days." Daniel 12:9-13.

The 1,260 days of the second half of the Tribulation begins when the Antichrist breaks the seven-year treaty with Israel, occupies the third Jewish Temple, and sets up an idol of himself as the object of worship. This 1,260-day period ends when the Antichrist is defeated at the battle of Armageddon upon Jesus' return to Earth. Even as these events bring a conclusion to the Tribulation, there are still more preparations to do in the first seventy-five days of the Millennium.

What is to happen in the first seventy-five days of Jesus' rule of the Earth? Dr. J. Vernon McGee said in his 1991 commentary on Daniel:

"Another series of days is given to us here with no other explanation than blessed is he who waits til the 1,335 days. No one has an interpretation of this. It is sealed until the time of the end."

Daniel was told to seal the prophecy for *"the words are closed up and sealed till the time of the end."* when the Millennium is near. Now that we are in the last days before the Lord's return, the meaning of these days is becoming clear to Bible prophecy students. The first 75 days of Jesus' reign will be divided into two periods of thirty (1290 minus 1260) and forty-five days (1335 minus 1290).

The Thirty Days of Cleansings:

The Word of God is meticulously accurate. For three and a half years, the statue of the Antichrist had desecrated the Temple. Also, the priests who are to serve in the Millennial Temple had not been consecrated. A similar situation happened in the days of King Hezekiah.

"For the king had taken counsel, and his princes, and all the congregation in Jerusalem, to keep the Passover in the second month. For they could not keep it at that time, because the priests had not sanctified themselves sufficiently, neither had the people gathered themselves together to Jerusalem. And the thing pleased the king and all the congregation." 2 Chronicles 2:2-4.

King Hezekiah said that there could be no Passover worship in the temple because there was a need to consecrate the priests, a process that would take 30 days. This is a beautiful picture of why an additional 30 days will be necessary for God's people to prepare themselves to rule and reign with Christ.

So adding these additional 30 days to Daniel's 1260 days will bring us to the prophesied 1290 days of Daniel's prophecy. Besides the priests being consecrated for service in the Temple, the Temple itself must be cleansed. Part of this cleansing is the removal of the "Abomination of Desolation."

> *"And deceiveth them that dwell on the earth by the means of those miracles which he had power to do in the sight of the beast; saying to them that dwell on the earth, that they should make an image to the beast, which had the wound by a sword, and did live. And he had power to give life unto the image of the beast, that the image of the beast should both speak, and cause that as many as would not worship the image of the beast should be killed." Revelation 13:14-15.*

When Solomon built the First Temple in Jerusalem, the sacrifice of an innumerable amount of sheep and oxen sanctified it. They sprinkled the blood of these animals on the furniture and instruments of worship. God accepted this sanctification by entering the Temple in a cloud that drove everyone else out. The Shekinah Glory of God dwelt in the Holy of Holies until the sin of people and their leaders caused Him to return to heaven, as recorded in the book of Ezekiel.

> *"And it came to pass, when the priests were come out of the holy place: (for all the priests that were present were sanctified, and did not then wait by*

course: Also the Levites which were the singers, all of them of Asaph, of Heman, of Jeduthun, with their sons and their brethren, being arrayed in white linen, having cymbals and psalteries and harps, stood at the east end of the altar, and with them an hundred and twenty priests sounding with trumpets:) It came even to pass, as the trumpeters and singers were as one, to make one sound to be heard in praising and thanking the LORD; and when they lifted up their voice with the trumpets and cymbals and instruments of music, and praised the LORD, saying, For he is good; for his mercy endureth for ever: that then the house was filled with a cloud, even the house of the LORD; So that the priests could not stand to minister by reason of the cloud: for the glory of the LORD had filled the house of God." 2 Chronicles 5:11-14.

A similar event may occur when Jesus the Messiah cleanses the Temple, with His own blood, from all traces of the desecration made by the Antichrist. Also, as part of the cleansing, Jesus will judge the Antichrist, the counterfeit son of God, and the False Prophet, the counterfeit Holy Spirit, for their rebellion and deception of man. God will cast them alive into the Lake of Fire. This fulfills the prophecy of Isaiah 14:20, which declares that the body of the Antichrist will never be buried.

Cleansing of the land will be during the first years in the Olam Haba.

"Several very specific comments are made concerning the cleansing of the land of the weapons of the Battle of Armageddon and the dead. The people of Israel will spend seven years gathering the weapons and burning them. Ezek 39:9 states that Israel will use defeated Gog's weapons for fuel for seven years after the battle. Modern weapons are made from a type of material called Lignite that is used in coke ovens. Lignite is a

variety of coal, intermediate in quality between peat and bituminous coal. Geologically Lignite is of comparative origin. It shows a distinct fibrous or woody structure that has a high content (52-62%) of volatile matter. It is stronger than steel, very elastic, and burns better than coal. A Dutchman in Ter-Appel founded this material. Israel imported coal from South Africa (2016), which will not be needed after the war. The possibility exists that Israel would not need to burn any kind of fuel after Moshiach sets up the Messianic Kingdom. Ezek 39:9-10: And they that dwell in the cities of Israel shall go forth and shall set on fire and burn the weapons, both the shields and the bucklers, the bows and the arrows, and the handstaves, and the spears, and they shall burn them with fire seven years: So that they shall take no wood out of the field, neither cut down any out of the forests; for they shall burn the weapons with fire: and they shall spoil those that spoiled them, and rob those that robbed them, saith the Lord HaShem." Prof. (Dr.) WA. Liebenberg.

The 45 days of Governing Preparation:

The other 45 days will be used as Christ judges the nations and their people and determines who are qualified to enter his glorious kingdom. For the first thousand years, the Lake of Fire will be inhabited by the Antichrist and the False Prophet by themselves. Satan, the counterfeit of God the Father, will be incarcerated in the bottomless pit, '*his fifth abode.*'

"And I saw an angel come down from heaven, having the key of the bottomless pit and a great chain in his hand. And he laid hold on the dragon, that old serpent, which is the Devil, and Satan, and bound him a thousand years, And cast him into the bottomless pit, and shut him up, and set a seal upon him, that he should deceive the nations no more, till the thousand years should

be fulfilled: and after that, he must be loosed a little season." Revelation 20:1-3.

The word used here for the *angel* that will bind Satan refers to one of the lowest celestial order. The duration of Satan's confinement will be one thousand years. Satan will be confined to the abyss, the temporary place of imprisonment of fallen angels. He will no longer be free to do his work of deception among nations and individuals. When his sentence is finished, he will be released for a short time to test individuals that have been born during the Millennium.

Jesus' Judgment of Anti-Semites:

Though many Gentiles will die during the Tribulation, and the gentle armies will suffer slaughter in the Campaign of Armageddon, a number will still survive. God will gather all the survivors for the sheep and goat judgment, as described in two passages of Scripture.

> ***"For, behold, in those days, and in that time, when I shall bring again the captivity of Judah and Jerusalem, I will also gather all nations, and will bring them down into the valley of Jehoshaphat, and will plead with them there for my people and for my heritage Israel, whom they have scattered among the nations, and parted my land. And they have cast lots for my people; and have given a boy for a harlot, and sold a girl for wine, that they might drink." Joel 3:1-3.***

This judgment is in conjunction with the final restoration of the nation of Israel. God will gather all the Gentiles into the Valley of Jehoshaphat. This judgment resulting in the destiny of eternal life or eternal hell has to be of individuals. The word translated *nations* also means *Gentiles*. God will judge all Gentiles based on their treatment of the Jews during the Great Tribulation. The sins listed are: scattering the Jews in the middle of the tribulation, parting the land during the Campaign of Armageddon, selling the Jews into slavery (see Zachariah 14:1-2). Each Gentile living at the end of the Tribulation will be judged based on his participation or refusal in these deeds. Matthew twenty-five gives the results of this judgment.

> *"When the Son of man shall come in his glory, and all the holy angels with him, then shall he sit upon the throne of his glory: And before him shall be gathered all nations: and he shall separate them one from another, as a shepherd divideth his sheep from the goats: And he shall set the sheep on his right hand, but the goats on the left. Then shall the King say unto them on his right hand, Come, ye blessed of my Father, inherit the kingdom prepared for you from the foundation of the world: For I was an hungered, and ye gave me meat: I was thirsty, and ye gave me drink: I was a stranger, and ye took me in: Naked, and ye clothed me: I was sick, and ye visited me: I was in prison, and ye came unto me. Matthew 25:31-40.*

The pro-Semites are those who give help to the Jews during the Great Tribulation, a time when it will be dangerous to do so. During this time, the Jews will have to flee into the wilderness, taking nothing with them, allowing the Sheep people to provide food and clothing and shelter. They will visit Jews in prison and perform other acts of kindness, and because of these acts, they will be allowed to enter the Messianic Kingdom. They will attain to the 1,335th day and be the ones who will populate Gentile nations in the Messianic Age.

> *"Then shall he say also unto them on the left hand, Depart from me, ye cursed, into everlasting fire, prepared for the devil and his angels: For I was an hungered, and ye gave me no meat: I was thirsty, and ye gave me no drink: I was a stranger, and ye took me not in: naked, and ye clothed me not: sick, and in prison, and ye visited me not. Then shall they also answer him, saying, Lord, when saw we thee an hungered, or athirst, or a stranger, or naked, or sick, or in prison, and did not minister unto thee? Then shall he answer them, saying, Verily I say unto you, Inasmuch as ye did it not to one of the least of these, ye did it not to me. And these shall go away into everlasting punishment: but the righteous into life eternal." Matthew 25:41-46.*

The anti-Semites, who will aid the Antichrist in his destruction of the Jews, will be killed and sent to hell. They are the ones who will fail to attain the1,335th day and consequently lose out on the millennial blessings. This judgment is not for determining the eternal state of individuals but is solely a judgment of the Gentiles on earth based on how they treated the Jewish people and Israel.

"The goats will be sent to hell, whereas the sheep will not only enter the kingdom, but they will also inherit eternal life. Is there salvation, then, based on their works, be they anti-Semitic or pro-Semitic? Not at all. The Scriptures make it quite clear that salvation is always by grace through faith totally apart from works. During the tribulation, the Jews will become the dividing line for those who are believers and those who are not. Only believers will dare to violate the rules of the Antichrist and aid the Jews. Their pro-Semitic acts will be the result of their saved state. As James would say it, they will show their faith by their works. But the unbelievers will demonstrate their unbelief by their anti-Semitic acts. The judgment of the Gentiles, then, will determine who among the

Gentiles will be allowed to enter the messianic kingdom. Only believing Gentiles will be allowed, and the evidence of their faith will be their pro-Semitic works." Dr. Arnold Fruchtenbaum.

> **"What doth it profit, my brethren, though a man say he hath faith, and have not works? Can faith save him? If a brother or sister be naked, and destitute of daily food, And one of you say unto them, Depart in peace, be ye warmed and filled; notwithstanding ye give them not those things which are needful to the body; what doth it profit? Even so, faith, if it hath not works, is dead, being alone. Yea, a man may say, Thou hast faith, and I have works: show me thy faith without thy works, and I will show thee my faith by my works." James 2:14-18.**

The Marriage Supper of the Lamb:

> *"Let us be glad and rejoice, and give honour to him: for the marriage of the Lamb is come, and his wife hath made herself ready. And to her was granted that she should be arrayed in fine linen, clean and white: for the fine linen is the righteousness of saints. Revelation 19:7-8.*

Scripture describes the relationship between Christ and the Church as a marriage. Christ is the Bridegroom, and the Church is the Bride. The Bible describes the Church as the virgin bride awaiting the coming of her heavenly bridegroom. While she waits, she keeps herself pure, unstained by the world.

The ancient Hebrew wedding takes place in three phases, as illustrated in the three aspects of marriage in the Bible.

Phase 1: Signing the *"Ketubbah"* contract (Creating the marriage bond)

The bride would choose her husband, and her father would sign a legal contract with the groom called a *"Ketubbah."*

Once this agreement is signed, the couple is 100% married but do not have sex yet.

As individuals living during the Church Age come to salvation, they become a part of the Church, the Bride of Christ, betrothed to the divine bridegroom.

In past times young children were often married (arraigned marriage) but did not consummate until they were of mature age.

Phase 2: The *"Chuppah."* consummation.

It could up to seven years for the groom to raise the money as set out in the Ketubbah contract. When a home is established, he notifies the father of the bride, who then sets a date to consummate the marriage at the bride's house.

The bride waits with her maidens for the arrival of the groom and his companions.

The couple enters the Chuppah room and consummates the marriage while the companions of the bride and groom wait and celebrate outside or in the next room.

The groom hands the bloodied "proof of virginity cloth" to the witnesses chosen by the bride's parents, who then give it to the bride for safekeeping.

The bridegroom, Jesus Christ, will come to claim His bride at the Rapture and takes the bride to Heaven, the father's house, where he has prepared a place to live. The actual wedding takes place in Heaven sometime after the Rapture of the Church.

Jim Zeigler

Phase 3: The wedding feast.

After consummation, the entire wedding party walks to the house of the groom in a procession for a wedding feast.

After the wedding feast, the couple has completed the ancient ritual of marriage.

Prof. (Dr.) W. A. Liebenberg views the marriage and supper as the fulfillment of the last three Hebrew feast days.

"Prophetic View of the Last Three Festivals:

"Prophetically, the Feast of Trumpets is, without a doubt, tied to the coming stealing of the bride strictly according the Ancient Hebrew Wedding Tradition. After the Feast of Trumpets (Rosh HaShanah) and then Atonement (Yom Kippur) takes place. This Feast of Yom Kippur will find its prophetic fulfillment when the bride will appear before the Bema, where our works will be tested for our crown rewards, and where the "at-one-ment" between Groom and bride will take place. The Feast of Tabernacles, called Sukkot in Hebrew, will find its prophetic fulfillment when we will Tabernacle (Sukkot) with YHWH away from our normal dwelling place for a shevuah, a period of seven.

The Various Names for Rosh Hashanah:

The following are all the different names used to describe the first day of the seventh month in the Biblical calendar:

- *Rosh HaShanah (New Year for Sabbaticals)*
- *Yom Teruah (The Day of the Awakening Blast or The Day of the Awakening Shout)*
- *Feast of Trumpets*
- *Yom Hadim (Day of Judgment)*

- *Yom HaZikkaron (Day of Remembrance)*
- *Yom HaKeseh (Day of the Hiding or Hidden Day)*

Rosh Hashanah Has and Always Will Be Associated with a Wedding:
Many ask, "Why do we associate the Feast of Trumpets with the
gathering of the bride?" Well, as said, another name for Rosh HaShanah
is Yom Teruah, or simply, "day of the awakening blast." The coronation
of the King, the resurrection of the dead, and the wedding of the Messiah
are among the many themes associated with Rosh HaShanah.

To add to this, Rosh HaShanah is also known as the "Day of our
Concealment." It is interesting to note that the bride and groom in the
Ancient Hebrew Wedding Tradition are concealed for one shavuah in
the chuppah (bridal chamber).

As said, this Feast of Yom Kippur (Day of Atonement) will find
its prophetic fulfillment when believers, Y'shua's bride will appear
before Y'shua's Bema where our works will be tested for our rewards
which are queen crowns, and where the "at-one-ment" will take place.
It is important to note that the bride will need a crown when she
sits on her throne as queen. The Sukkot Feast will find its prophetic
fulfillment when we will Tabernacle with YHWH AWAY from our
NORMAL dwelling place for a shavuah, a period of seven. The only
sukkah (tabernacle/booth) known in Scripture where the NT bride can
enter for a shavuah (period of seven), away from her normal dwelling
place—planet earth—is the New Jerusalem City.

The Feast of Tabernacles demands a person to leave your normal
house dwelling for one shavuah to stay in a sukkah, and she, as the bride,
will get married at the same time. If the New Jerusalem City is not the
sukkah for the future fulfilment for the Feast of Tabernacles, then what
other place and future event provides both a 1) sukkah and 2) a shavuah
for the believers to fulfill YHWH's festival conditions in His 'plan of
redemption' as laid out in His Seven Festivals in Leviticus chapter 23?"
Prof. (Dr.) WA Liebenberg.

The marriage supper of the Lamb apparently takes place on

earth during the 75-day interval between the end of the tribulation and at the beginning of the Millennial Kingdom.

There was no "wedding ceremony" in the synagogue in the first century, performed under a canopy where the bride and groom would hold hands and say, "I do" before an audience of friends and family. This didn't develop for hundreds of years after Jesus died on the cross as the Passover lamb for the sins of humanity.

> *"And he saith unto me, Write, Blessed are they which are called unto the marriage supper of the Lamb. And he saith unto me, These are the true sayings of God." Revelation 19:9.*

The invitation to the marriage supper is to the Old Testament and Tribulation saints who comprise the friends of the bridegroom.

"The result of the invitation is the resurrection and the wedding feast, which will also last at least seven days, and will either include the 75-day interval or may inaugurate the Messianic Kingdom itself for his first seven days-perhaps the more likely scenario since the wedding feast parable was connected with the kingdom. One such wedding feast parable is found in Matthew 22:1-14." Dr. Arnold Fruchtenbaum.

> *"And Jesus answered and spake unto them again by parables, and said, The kingdom of heaven is like unto a certain king, which made a marriage for his son, And sent forth his servants to call them that were bidden to the wedding: and they would not come. Again, he sent forth other servants, saying, Tell them which are bidden, Behold, I have prepared my dinner: my oxen and my fatlings are killed, and all things are ready: come unto the marriage. But they made light of it, and went their ways, one to his farm, another to his merchandise: And the remnant*

*took his servants, and entreated them spitefully, and slew them. But when the king heard thereof, he was wroth: and he sent forth his armies, and destroyed those murderers, and burned up their city. Then saith he to his servants, The wedding is ready, but they which were bidden were not worthy. Go ye therefore into the highways, and as many as ye shall find, bid to the marriage. So those servants went out into the highways, and gathered together all as many as they found, both bad and good: and the wedding was furnished with guests. And when the king came in to see the guests, he saw there a man which had not on a wedding garment: And he saith unto him, Friend, how camest thou in hither not having a wedding garment? And he was speechless. Then said the king to the servants, Bind him hand and foot, and take him away, and cast him into outer darkness; there shall be weeping and gnashing of teeth. For many are called, but few are chosen."
Matthew 22:1-14.*

"*The point of the parable is that those who were originally bidden to the wedding feast, the Pharisees and the Jewish generation of Jesus day, will not partake of the feast of the kingdom do to their commitment of the unpardonable sin* [rejection of Jesus' blood sacrifice for their sins]. *However, the Jews of the tribulation generation will. But this will include only the believers, the unbelievers will be cast into outer darkness and excluded from the messianic kingdom.*" Arnold Fruchtenbaum.

Likewise, in the parable of the Wise and Foolish Virgins, (Mathew 25:1-13), the contrast is not between two types of believers, but between believers and unbelievers. The wise virgins, believers, had oil (a symbol of the Holy Spirit), while the foolish virgins do not. Thus the foolish ones are excluded from the wedding feast of the

Messiah, which is why the Lord said to them *Verily I say unto you, I know you not*, while the wise virgins went into the marriage feast.

Scripture suggests that there will be a double wedding feast. One for the Church as the bride of Jesus the Messiah and one for Israel as the remarried Wife of Jehovah.

Isaiah connects the resurrection with a feast in with the Kingdom as a double celebration.

> *"And in this mountain, shall the LORD of hosts make unto all people a feast of fat things, a feast of wines on the lees, of fat things full of marrow, of wines on the lees well refined. And he will destroy in this mountain the face of the covering cast over all people, and the veil that is spread over all nations. He will swallow up death in victory; and the Lord GOD will wipe away tears from off all faces; and the rebuke of his people shall he take away from off all the earth: for the LORD hath spoken it." Isaiah 25:6-8.*

These events lead to the thousand-year-long period of history the faithful look for–the Millennium or the Messianic Age.

Part Two

The Millennial Kingdom

3

Resurrection of Eden

"For, behold, I create new heavens and a new earth: and the former shall not be remembered, nor come into mind." Isaiah 65:17.

Isaiah announces the new heavens and new earth, but we should not confuse these with the new heaven and earth that John describes in Revelation twenty and twenty-one. What the prophet is describing is the Millennial renovation/restoration of this world to its original state. The earth's topography, climate, and the atmosphere remained as God created it until the flood in Noah's day, approximately 1,656 years later. However, when *"God saw that the wickedness of man was great in the earth, and that every imagination of the thoughts of his heart was only evil continually,"* He destroyed the earth with a worldwide flood that killed all His creation except those in Noah's ark of grace.

"In the six hundredth year of Noah's life, in the second month, the seventeenth day of the month, the same day were all the fountains of the great deep broken up, and the windows of heaven were opened. And the rain was upon the earth forty days and forty nights." Genesis 7:11-12.

Noah's world:

The antediluvian hydrologic cycle differed vastly from what we know today. On day two of creation, God separated the waters into two vast reservoirs. One reservoir of waters, the primordial deep, was below the firmament and the other above the firmament. The firmament, in this case comprising the atmospheric heavens or sky.

"And God said, Let there be a firmament in the midst of the waters, and let it divide the waters from the waters. And God made the firmament, and divided the waters which were under the firmament from the waters which were above the firmament: and it was so. And God called the firmament Heaven. And the evening and the morning were the second day. And God said, Let the waters under the heaven be gathered together unto one place, and let the dry land appear: and it was so. And God called the dry land Earth; and the gathering together of the waters called he Seas: and God saw that it was good." Genesis 1:6-8.

"The waters below the firmament became what is referred to as the 'great deep' or the 'great depths' of water. This was water in the liquid state, visible especially to the first land in the form of the antediluvian seas and rivers. These rivers were not produced by runoff from rainfall

but emerge through controlled fountains or springs evidently from deep-seated sources in or below the earth's crust.'" Henry M. Morris.

"The waters above the firmament constituted the vast vaporous canopy which maintained the earth as a beautiful greenhouse, preventing cold temperatures and therefore preventing wind and rainstorms. Being in the vapor state, it was invisible and fully transparent, but nevertheless contained vast quantities of water extending far out into space." Henry M. Morris.

The Bible explicitly attributes the flood to the bursting of the fountains of the great deep and the pouring down of torrential rains from the windows of heaven. How God accomplished these works is for a later discussion, but for now, all we need to know is that God caused the flood of Noah's day as a judgment for sinful man.

> *"And God saw that the wickedness of man was great in the earth, and that every imagination of the thoughts of his heart was only evil continually." Genesis 6:5.*

The world after the Tribulation:

At the end of the Tribulation, when the seventh bowl judgment is poured out upon the earth, a voice cries out from heaven, *"it is done"* because this brings an end to the tribulation judgments. The judgment includes convulsions of nature, including the most significant earthquake ever to occur in the history of planet Earth. This eruption of god's anger will cause major geographical changes to take place.

> *"Multitudes, multitudes in the valley of decision: for the day of the LORD is near in the valley of decision. The sun and the moon shall be darkened, and the stars shall withdraw their*

shining. The LORD also shall roar out of Zion, and utter his voice from Jerusalem; and the heavens and the earth shall shake: but the LORD will be the hope of his people, and the strength of the children of Israel. So shall ye know that I am the LORD your God dwelling in Zion, my holy mountain: then shall Jerusalem be holy, and there shall no strangers pass through her any more." Joel 3:14-17.

The author believes that this last judgment will prepare the earth for the Messiah's 'Earth Restoration Program.' The great earthquake will separate the waters of the Earth, restoring the fountains in the deep, raising the land upward, purifying the waters into lakes and spring-fed streams, and rivers, and restoring the protective vapor canopy over the earth.

"And there were voices, and thunders, and lightnings; and there was a great earthquake, such as was not since men were upon the earth, so mighty an earthquake, and so great. And every island fled away, and the mountains were not found." Revelation 16:18&20.

"God will also cause great rearrangements of the firmament that will both enhance the cosmetics of the planet and provide vast, new inhabitable land area. Earth presently has an enormous 140 million-square-mile land area hiding under the oceans. These future masses include mountains higher than Mount Everest and chasms deeper than the Grand Canyon---realms to provide the most pleasant scenery. All present faults and strains in the Earth's crust will be relieved during that series of explosive quakes, and when the dust settles, our planet will be entirely earthquake free." George Otis Sr.

God may also, at that time, restore the axis of the earth to its original plane, thus stopping the seasonal variations of temperature. God has altered the universe's timing and orbits occasionally several times, as is recorded in the Bible.

Known as axial tilt, where a planet's vertical axis is tilted a certain number of degrees towards the ecliptic of the object it orbits (in this case, the Sun). Such a tilt results in there being a difference in how much sunlight reaches a given point on the surface during a year. With Earth, the axis is tilted towards the ecliptic of the Sun at approximately 23.44° (or 23.439281° to be exact).

Besides variations in temperature, seasonal changes also result in changes to the biannual cycle. In the Summer, the days last longer, and the Sun climbs higher in the sky. In Winter, the days become shorter, and the Sun is lower in the sky. In northern temperate latitudes, the Sun rises north of true east during the summer solstice, and sets north of true west, reversing in the winter. The Sun rises south of true east in the summer for the southern temperate zone and sets south of true west.

"The four seasons can be determined by the solstices (the point of maximum axial tilt toward or away from the Sun) and the equinoxes (when the direction of tilt and the Sun are perpendicular). In the northern hemisphere, winter solstice occurs around December 21st, summer solstice around June 21st, spring equinox around March 20th, and autumnal equinox on or about September 22nd or 23rd. In the southern hemisphere, the situation is reversed, with the summer and winter solstices exchanged and the spring and autumnal equinox dates swapped."

"The angle of the Earth's tilt is relatively stable over long periods of time. However, Earth's axis does undergo a slight irregular motion known as nutation*—a rocking, swaying, or nodding motion (like a gyroscope)—that has a period of 18.6 years. Earth's axis is also subject to a slight wobble (like a spinning top), which is causing its orientation to change over time".* Harry Rimmer.

God also added about a day for Joshua to fight the Amorites and turned the sundial back ten degrees for Hezekiah.

"Then spake Joshua to the LORD in the day when the LORD delivered up the Amorites before the children of Israel, and he said in the sight of Israel, Sun, stand thou still upon Gibeon; and thou, Moon, in the valley of Ajalon. And the sun stood still, and the moon stayed, until the people had avenged themselves upon their enemies. Is not this written in the book of Jasher? So the sun stood still in the midst of heaven and hasted not to go down about a whole day. And there was no day like that before it or after it, that the LORD hearkened unto the voice of a man: for the LORD fought for Israel." Joshua 10:12-14.

"As to how this was effected, the closing words of vs. 13 'and hasted not to go down about a whole day,' suggest that the relative positions of the sun and the earth did not hold still but merely slowed in their change. This means that the earth simply slowed, in its speed of rotation on its axis, approximately to half that of normal. This did not affect the speed of movement around the sun of the rest of the solar system, which complicating factors have been mentioned in criticism by those advocating other explanations," Leon Wood.

"There have been stories circulating about reports of a 'missing day' in ancient Egyptian, Chinese, and Hindu sources. There is also the story of a Yale astronomer who found that the earth was twenty-four hours out of schedule: Another professor at Yale, Dr. Totten, suggested the astronomer read the Bible starting at the beginning and going as far as necessary, to see if the Bible could account for the missing time. When he came to the account of the long day of Joshua, the astronomer rechecked the figures and found that at the time of Joshua, there were only twenty-three hours and twenty minutes lost. His skepticism justified, he decided that the Bible was not the Word of God because there was a mistake by forty minutes. Professor Totten showed him that the Bible account does not say twenty-four hours, but rather about the space of an entire day.

On reading farther, the astronomer found that God, through the prophet Isaiah and in answer to Hezekiah's prayer, promised to add fifteen years to his life. To confirm this promise, the shadow of the sundial was turned back ten degrees. Ten degrees on a sundial is forty minutes on the face of a clock. When he found his day of missing time accounted for in the Bible, the astronomer bowed his head in worship of its Author, saying, "Lord, I believe!" Harry Rimmer

God's Creation Restored:

The God who created the Heavens and Earth in one week. He is also capable of resurrecting the world to its original designed structure.

> *"And God said, Let the earth bring forth grass, the herb yielding seed, and the fruit tree yielding fruit after his kind, whose seed is in itself, upon the earth: and it was so. And the earth brought forth grass, and herb yielding seed after his kind, and the tree yielding fruit, whose seed was in itself, after his kind: and God saw that it was good. And the evening and the morning were the third day." Genesis 1:11-13.*

Just as Jesus did in Genesis on the third day of Creation, He will again restore the vegetation to its original luscious status. God will resurrect and restore the three classes of plant life: grasses, herbs, and trees. The term 'grass' should include all spreading ground-covering vegetation; 'herbs' contain all the bushes and shrubs, 'trees' comprises all large woody plants, including fruit-bearing trees. This resurrection would also include vegetation that is no longer in existence on the planet restored according to each species own DNA genetic code.

And God said, Let there be lights in the firmament of the heaven to divide the day from the night; and let them be for signs, and for seasons, and for days, and years: And let them be for lights in the firmament of the heaven to give light upon the earth: and it was so. And God made two great lights; the greater light to rule the day, and the lesser light to rule the night: he made the stars also. And God set them in the firmament of the heaven to give light upon the earth, And to rule over the day and over the night, and to divide the light from the darkness: and God saw that it was good. And the evening and the morning were the fourth day. Genesis 1:14-19.

Just as God had created the Sun, Moon, and Stars to give light on the earth and guidance to man, he will once again restore the heavens to their former glory by showing the story of salvation in the Zodiac.

"The gospel in the stars is just another example of God's original message being perverted by Satan and sinful men. Instead of trusting in Christ to which the stars point so gloriously, people who practice astrology trust the stars themselves. The modern corruption of astrology expresses the idea that some mysterious, magical, and supernatural powers emanate from the houses of the zodiac, which affect and control destiny and lives. That is a lie of Satan, which will destroy every soul that believes it. Instead, what God put in the stars is a glorious sky painting of Jesus Christ as the Lord of glory."

"At the time of the building of the tower of Babel, this was corrupted into astrology. Thus, instead of these being signs of God and his salvation by which we should worship God, they were changed into deities, and people began to worship the sun, the moon, the planets, and the stars." Dr. D. James Kennedy.

When we look at the twelve signs from a Christian perspective, we can see the story of redemption.

Virgo-the seed of the woman, speaks of Christ as the incarnate son of God will be 100% God and 100% man.

Libra- the required price paid, relates to Christ as the Redeemer who paid the full price for our salvation.

Scorpio- the mortal conflict, declares Christ was wounded for our transgressions and bruised by the victory over Satan.

Sagittarius- the ultimate triumph, portrays Christ, the God-man, as the victory over sin and Satan.

Capricorn- life out of death, illustrates that through Christ's death or our sins, we are made spiritually alive.

Aquarius- blessing out of victory, speaks of the joy of God's Spirit poured out on his people as the fruit of Jesus' victory.

Pisces- deliverance out of bondage, foretells of God's deliverance of people of all nations from the slavery of sin into the glorious light of his love through the preaching of the gospel.

Aries- Jesus' glory out of humiliation, illustrates how, although Christ was humbled and slain as the Lamb of God, He has been raised from the dead and made the ruler of all creation.

Taurus- His glorious coming, foretells the Christ will come in judgment like a rampaging bull upon the sinful world.

Gemini- His union with his bride, speaks of Christ's fellowship with his people in his eternal kingdom.

Cancer- His possessions held secure, assures us of God's fulfillment of his promise that he will have a great kingdom filled with a multitude of people from every race, tribe, and nation.

Leo- His enemies destroyed, prophetically assures us that Jesus Christ will be victorious over sin, the world, and Satan.

Thus the heavens will declare, through all the Millennium, the old, old story of glad tidings unto men.

I also think God will remove all of man's space trash left in the heavens that hinder the exploration of God's universe. God will restore the lights in the sky to their original purposes *"for signs, and for seasons, and for days, and years:"*

"It is interesting that the stars are mentioned as of only minor importance relative to the sun. *'He made the stars also.'* Even though stars are incomparably bigger than the earth, and many of them even larger than our sun, there is much of simpler structure than the earth. A star is mostly hydrogen and helium, complexly quite simple; whereas the structure of the earth is of great complexity, perfectly and uniquely designed for living creatures. Complexity and organization are much more meaningful measures of significance than mere size!" Henry M. Morris.

> **"And God said, Let the waters bring forth abundantly the moving creature that hath life, and fowl that may fly above the earth in the open firmament of heaven. And God created great whales and every living creature that moveth, which the waters brought forth abundantly, after their kind, and every winged fowl after his kind: and God saw that it was good. And God blessed them, saying, Be fruitful, and multiply, and fill the waters in the seas, and let fowl multiply in the earth. And the evening and the morning were the fifth day." Genesis 1:20-23.**

Next, God will put His blessing on the sea creatures and the fowls of the air. Genesis 1:20 refers to all kinds of marine animals: invertebrates, vertebrates, and reptiles. Besides the animals of the hydrosphere, there are also animals of the atmosphere: birds to fly in, literally, the space of the firmament of heaven.

"The first animal specifically mentioned as a product of this act of creation where the great whales, or great sea-monsters, as most translations render the Hebrew word 'tannin.' It is significant, however, that the same word is frequently translated dragon. Evidently, the term *includes all large sea-creatures, even monsters of the past that are now extinct. Frequent references to dragons in the Bible, as well as in the early records and traditions of most of the nations of antiquity, certainly cannot be shrugged off as mere fairytales. Most probably, they represent memories of dinosaurs handed down by tribal ancestors encountered them before they became extinct."* Henry M. Morris.

God will resurrect all the wild animal species that are now extinct and change them to the friendly creatures we want to love and pet. God will remove the fear of between man and creatures.

> ***"And God said, Let the earth bring forth the living creature after his kind, cattle, and creeping thing, and beast of the earth after his kind: and it was so. And God made the beast of the earth after his kind, and cattle after their kind, and every thing that creepeth upon the earth after his kind: and God saw that it was good." Genesis 1:24-25.***

God will resurrect the extinct species of cattle, creeping things, and beasts of the earth. The term beasts of the earth include large mammals such as lions and elephants, and probably also giant extinct reptiles such as dinosaurs. Creeping things comprises the insects' smaller reptiles and perhaps even more amphibians and many small mammals such as moles, rats, mice.

"All three categories of land animals were made simultaneously, as is evident from the inverted order of the listing in verses 24 and 25. Once again, it is obvious that there is not the slightest correlation with the imaginary evolutionary order (that is, insects, then amphibians, then reptiles, then all mammals). As a matter of fact, evolution places insects, amphibians, and land reptiles all before the birds that Genesis says was made the day before.

There is no evolutionary struggle for existence among these animals either, ***"God saw that it was good."*** *Neither could one kind evolved into a different kind because God made each category* ***"after his kind."***

"All these land animals were said to have been 'brought forth' from the earth or ground. That is, their bodies were composed of the same elements as the earth, and when they died, they would go back to the earth. They also all had 'souls' because they were said to be 'living creatures.' In this respect, they were like air and water animals (Genesis 1:21) and also like man (Genesis 2:7)." Henry M. Morris.

They all have a self-awareness that plants don't have, but man does. Try going after your roses and dog with a knife, and you will see the dog will become defensive, but the rose will not because the dog knows of his existence and will try to defend his life.

"Among the intentions of Jesus was to show people what Eden had been like, and what life with God would be. In God's family and God's rule, there will be no disease and no physical imperfections. There will also be no hostile powers. God's ultimate kingdom is bigger than a garden, wider than Israel. The kingdom will be global. It will include all nations. And it will be everything Eden was --- heaven on earth." Michael S. Heiser.

Rebuilding during the Millennium will be accomplished both by God's supernatural acts and also by human endeavors. We will witness all the restorations of the world as it is progressively restored to its original perfection.

A Whole Universe to Explore:

"For as the heavens are higher than the earth, so are my ways higher than your ways, and my thoughts than your thoughts." Isaiah 55:9.

The size of God's universe boggles the human mind. As God is infinite, having no beginning and no end, so too is his universe. No matter how powerful a microscope we create, we cannot find the smallest element of God's creation. And with the most powerful telescopes and can still not see the end of God's universe.

Light traveling at 186,000 miles per second takes a thousand years to cross our galaxy. Astrologers now claim there are more than a billion other galaxies. Each discovery of God's exotic cosmic mysteries boggles our minds.

Black holes in our universe exert such a massive pull that everything within a million miles is sucked inside of them and forever lost. Scientists theorize that at one time, they were massive bodies that have undergone gravitational collapse. Since there is an enormous pull that prevents even light from escaping, they can only be detected by x-ray. We can never see inside a black hole or know what happened because no form of energy can escape carrying the information.

Could these black holes out in space be the places that the Bible describes as outer darkness? Could one of them be the bottomless pit or the compartments of hell? No one knows.

We know that somewhere in the universe is a place of beautiful light that was spoken of by the apostles John and Paul. Lavished with priceless stones, gold, and crystal, it is God's office and residence and a place we call Heaven.

"Is not God in the height of heaven? and behold the height of the stars, how high they are!" Job 22:12.

God has made not only the earth but the entire universe for man's involvement. We must stretch our vision to encompass our millennial assignments in God's colossal realms during eternity.

"When I consider thy heavens, the work of thy fingers, the moon, and the stars, which thou hast ordained; What is man, that thou art mindful of him? And the son of man, that thou visitest him? For thou hast made him a little lower than the angels, and hast crowned him with glory and

honour. Thou madest him to have dominion over
the works of thy hands; thou hast put all things
under his feet:" Psalm 8:3-6.

I wonder what logistical problems interstellar travel would need to be resolved. If it takes light a thousand years to cross our galaxy, how would we ever get to the edges of God's creation? What is faster than light? The answer is the speed of thought! We will just have to *think there to be there.*

"He stretcheth out the north over the empty place,
and hangeth the earth upon nothing." Job 26:7.

4

New World Capital

"But be ye glad and rejoice for ever in that which I create: for behold, I create Jerusalem a rejoicing, and her people a joy. And I will rejoice in Jerusalem, and joy in my people: and the voice of weeping shall be no more heard in her, nor the voice of crying." Isiah 65:18-19.

The New Landscape for Jerusalem & Israel:

When Jesus, the Messiah, returns great topographical changes will occur in the land of Israel. Jerusalem will raise as the highest mountain in the world.

"The earth will be changed at the beginning of the Messianic Age. There are many references, to specific areas that are targeted for reconstruction, but the most devastating changes on the face of the earth will occur through Israel and Lebanon.

Jim Zeigler

*After the changes, a riverbed will exist in its centre from the Dead Sea to the Gulf of Aqaba. All of these fantastic horizontal and vertical adjustments in the valley will produce a new Jordan River system, a system planned, prophesied, and created by HaShem (**Hebrew for "The Name," the reference to YHWH**). One will discover the New River system slowly forming into the headwaters of the Jordan River. Systems will begin in Turkey, flow across Syria into northern Israel, pass southward through the old Jordan River Valley, move slowly through the Idumean rift, and finally empty into the Gulf of Aqaba. The Euphrates River will be diverted, and the Arabah Fault will be opened. Gradually what we now know as the Dead Sea will become an inland lake as most its salts content drains southward into the Red Sea, and the deserts of Israel will blossom as the rose. After the changes are made to the earth, it will be calm and quiet. The Prophet Zechariah (14:10) says: "**All the land shall be turned as a plain from Geba to Rimmon south of Jerusalem, and it shall be lifted up and inhabited in her place, from Benjamin's gate unto the place of the first gate, unto the corner gate, and from the tower of Hananeel unto the king's wine-presses.**"*

*Because of its exacting detail as to the section of land that would be lifted up, this is perhaps the most remarkable geological prophecy in the TaNaCh (**The Hebrew Bible**). We are advised that along a line from Geba to Rimmon HaShem intends to produce a fantastic geological transformation of the landscape. When this violent transformational action is completed, there will be a plain like zone from Geba to Rimmon, and at the same time, a lifting movement will have elevated the two western hills of Jerusalem. This Scripture indicates that the land immediately to the west of the line from Geba to Rimmon will be "lifted up" to a higher elevation, while the land immediately to the east of this line will be lowered to form what appears "as a plain." The lifting of the land from Geba to Rimmon will include the city of Jerusalem. Those Jerusalem sections west of the Tyropoeon Valley will be lifted up, and those sections to the east will collapse into a plain. The Prophet Zechariah knew nothing about structural weaknesses in the* *crust of the earth, nor did anyone else in his day. There was only one being who did, HaShem, who made the earth. The same God, who inspired Zechariah to write, placed a structural weakness in the crust of the earth from Geba to Rimmon long before Zechariah was born. It was an appropriate type of weakness; one that went up and down. It is only from within the later part of the twentieth century that men have begun to understand how this particular type of crustal mechanism works."* Prof. (Dr.) WA Liebenberg.

Israel's promised land:

God as the creator of earth holds the title deed to the promised land. He transferred the ownership to Abraham, Isaac, and Jacob and their descendants forever.

> *"And it came to pass, that, when the sun went down, and it was dark, behold a smoking furnace, and a burning lamp that passed between those pieces. In the same day the LORD made a covenant with Abram, saying, Unto thy seed have I given this land, from the river of Egypt unto the great river, the river Euphrates: The Kenites, and the concerts, and the Kadmonites, And the Hittites, and the Perizzites, and the Rephaims, And the Amorites, and the Canaanites, and the Girgashites, and the Jebusites." Genesis 15:17-21.*

Genesis 15 God makes a covenant with Abraham and confirms it with the practice of dividing sacrificial animals to create a path for the contracting parties to pass through. However, in this case, only God passes through the carcasses, making this a unilateral covenant with God. The promise is made by God and will be performed by God.

The land given by God to Abraham and his descendants extended from the Nile River of Egypt to the Euphrates River in modern-day Iraq and from Hamath, northeast of Damascus, to Kadesh in the South (Ezekiel 48:1-29).

"The promised land includes all of the land Israel now owns, plus Judea and Samaria, Gaza, parts of Egypt, Syria, Lebanon, and Iraq." John Hagee.

Although the land has been occupied by several Gentile conquerors and even renamed Palestine by the Roman Emperor Hadrian, the title deed belongs to the descendants of Abraham, Israel.

"The Covenant God made with King David gave him a royal dynasty that would rule over His Kingdom forever. When Jesus Christ, the Son of David, sits on His throne Temple Mount in Jerusalem during the millennial reign, this covenant will be fulfilled. Our God is the promise keeper!" John Hagee.

Chosen by God as the place of worship:

The book of Genesis tells us about a conflict surrounding Sodom in which four kings defeated five kings and captured all their goods and people.

> *"And they took all the goods of Sodom and Gomorrah, and all their victuals, and went their way. And they took Lot, Abram's brother's son, who dwelt in Sodom, and his goods, and departed." Genesis 14:11-12.*

Abraham took the 318 servants from his household and rescued Lot, his nephew, and all the stuff captured by Chedorlaomer and the kings who *were* with him. On his return home, Melchizedek king of Salem met Abraham.

"And the king of Sodom went out to meet him after his return from the slaughter of Chedorlaomer, and of the kings that were with him, at the valley of Shaveh, which is the king's dale. And Melchizedek king of Salem brought forth bread and wine: and he was the priest of the most high God. And he blessed him, and said, Blessed be Abram of the most high God, possessor of heaven and earth: And blessed be the most high God, which hath delivered thine enemies into thy hand. And he gave him tithes of all." **Genesis 14:17-20.**

Melchizedek, in the Old Testament, a figure of importance in the biblical tradition because he was both king and priest, was of Jerusalem, and was revered by Abraham, who paid a tithe to him. Melchizedek is more of a title than a personal name. The title comes from two Hebrew words, the first being Melek meaning "king," and the second, which is Tsedeq or "righteousness" (Strong's #H4442). In Genesis 14, this person is labeled a priest and the king of Salem (the word Salem means "peace"). Salem in King's David's time was changed to Jerusalem. Salem is also an old name for the city of Jerusalem, being the place of the Most High God, *El Elyon*. Jesus is described in Hebrews as being a priest after the order of Melchizedek.

"Through the Order of Melchizedek, God intended, in advance, that the Old Covenant Levitical priesthood last for only a short time (Hebrews 7:11 - 12, 9 - 10) and be replaced. This is why the Biblical appearance of Melchizedek (Genesis 14:18 - 20) occurred many decades before Levi (Abraham's great-grandson) was born." www.biblestudy.org.

Chosen by God as the place of sacrifice:

God promised Abraham a son in his old age. And that son would be the father of many nations and bring blessing to the entire world. But after many years, Abraham's faith weakened, and he decided to help God fulfill his promise. So God had to reaffirm his faith.

> *"And it came to pass after these things, that God did tempt (test) Abraham, and said unto him, Abraham: and he said, Behold, here I am. And he said, Take now thy son, thine only son Isaac, whom thou lovest, and get thee into the land of Moriah; and offer him there for a burnt offering upon one of the mountains which I will tell thee of." Genesis 22:1-2*

God and two angels, while on the way to judge Sodom, stopped to give a hopeful message to Abraham. His son would begin a line of believers that would lead to the Saviour of the world. Ishmael was the son born to Sarah's slave, Hagar, when Abraham tried to get ahead of God's plan for a redeemer. Years later, Isaac, the son of God's promise, was born to Sarah in their old age.

God was testing Abraham's faith in Him, Abraham's love for Him. God needed to prove to Abraham that Abraham had the belief in God he would need to become the father of many nations.

> *"And Abraham rose up early in the morning, and saddled his ass, and took two of his young men with him, and Isaac his Son, and clave the wood for the burnt offering, and rose up, and went unto the place of which God had told him. Then on the third day Abraham lifted up his eyes, and saw the place afar off. And Abraham said unto his young men, Abide ye here with the ass;*

and I and the lad will go yonder and worship, and come again to you. And Abraham took the wood of the burnt offering, and laid it upon Isaac his Son; and he took the fire in his hand, and a knife; and they went, both of them together. (in agreement)" Genesis 22:3-6

Abraham started early the next morning with Isaac and two servants. He didn't argue with God about God's promise for Isaac's life. Isaac was in his late teens and could have overpowered his father, but in obedience obeyed and carried the wood.

They went, both of them together.

"And Isaac spake unto Abraham, his father, and said, My father: and he said, Here am I, my Son. And he said, Behold the fire and the wood: but where is the lamb for a burnt offering? And Abraham said, My Son, God will provide himself a lamb for a burnt offering: so they went both of them together." Genesis 22:7-8.

When Isaac asked, "Where is the Lamb?" His father said, *"God will provide himself a lamb for a burnt offering."*

"And if his offering be of the flocks, namely, of the sheep, or of the goats, for a burnt sacrifice; he shall bring it a male without blemish." Leviticus 1:10.

<u>*God will provide Himself, a lamb:*</u>

"And they came to the place which God had told him of; and Abraham built an altar there, and laid the wood in order, and bound Isaac his Son, and laid him on the altar upon the wood.

And Abraham stretched forth his hand, and took the knife to slay his Son." Genesis 22:9-10.

Abraham bound Isaac placed on the wood, and Abraham **"took the knife to slay his Son."** *This whole incident paints a picture of Jesus' death on the cross as our "Lamb of God, which takes away our sins."*

> **"And the Angel of the Lord called unto him out of heaven, and said, Abraham, Abraham: and he said, Here am I. And he said, Lay not thine hand upon the lad, neither do thou any thing unto him: for now I know that thou fearest God, seeing thou hast not withheld thy Son, thine only Son from me. And Abraham lifted up his eyes, and looked, and behold behind him a ram caught in a thicket <u>by his horns</u>: and Abraham went and took the <u>ram</u> and offered him up for a burnt offering in the stead of his Son. And Abraham called the name of that place Jehovahjireh: as it is said to this day, In the mount of the LORD it shall be seen." Genesis 22:11-14.**

Abraham's Faith was proven, and God showed that He would provide a sinless saviour, Jesus, as our sin sacrifice. The ram was acceptable because it was caught **"by his horns,"** the only way that lamb would not be marred.

> **"Your lamb shall be without blemish."**
> **Exodus 12:5**

Jacob's place of safety:

Abraham's grandson Jacob, when he was fleeing from his brother Esau in fear for his life on his flight to Syria, stopped in what was then called Luz to rest for the night. While he was sleeping, he dreamed of a staircase that reached to heaven. At the top of the staircase stood the Lord, who promised him that his descendants would possess the land on which he lay and that all the families of the earth would be blessed. When he awoke, he determined that he had been sleeping at the gate of heaven. The Bible records that Jacob renamed the place Bethel or the house of God.

"According to the late Rabbi Yehuda Getz, there were actually two Bethels and this particular one was what became known later as the Temple Mount in Jerusalem. It was the same place that Abraham had been led to in order to offer Isaac as an 'Olah' or burnt offering. Actually, the Scripture refers to this spot as "the place," or in Hebrew 'ha Makom'. According to rabbinic sources, we understand this place as being "the Lord." So, in other words, Abraham took Isaac to the place where the Lord is seen. (Genesis 22:14)'

"The book of Jasher confirms that 'the place' in Genesis 22 is the same place where Jacob saw the gate of heaven opened." Perry Stone.

> "And Jacob went forth continuing his road to Haran, and he came as far as Mount Moriah, and he tarried there all night near the city named Luz and the Lord appeared there unto Jacob on that night," Jasher 30:1.

David's Faith Corrected:

> "And Satan stood up against Israel, and provoked David to number Israel. (count his army) And David said to Joab and to the rulers of the people, Go, number Israel from Beersheba even to Dan; and bring the number of them to me, that I may know it. And Joab answered, The LORD make his people an hundred times so many more as they be: but, my lord the king,

> *are they not all my lord's servants? Why then doth my lord require this thing? Why will he be a cause of trespass to Israel? Nevertheless, the king's word prevailed against Joab. Wherefore Joab departed, and went throughout all Israel, and came to Jerusalem. And Joab gave the sum of the number of the people unto David. And all they of Israel were a thousand thousand and an hundred thousand men that drew sword: and Judah was four hundred threescore and ten thousand men that drew sword. But Levi and Benjamin counted he not among them: for the king's word was abominable to Joab." 1 Chronicles 1-6.*

David put faith in the size of his army and not in God. David asked Joab to number the men of war, and Joab reported an army of 1,570,000. From Israel,1,100,000 and Judah, 470,000. However, Joab, the head of the military, objected and did not finish the job. The tribes of Levi and Benjamin not counted.

> *"And God was displeased with this thing; therefore, he smote Israel. And David said unto God, I have sinned greatly because I have done this thing: but now, I beseech thee, do away the iniquity of thy servant; for I have done very foolishly. And the LORD spake unto Gad, David's seer, saying, Go and tell David, saying, Thus saith the LORD, I offer thee three things: choose thee one of them, that I may do it unto thee." 1 Chronicles 21:7-10.*

Sin, even after repentance, still has consequences.

"So Gad came to David, and said unto him, Thus saith the LORD, Choose thee Either three years' famine; or three months to be destroyed before thy foes, while that the sword of thine enemies overtaketh thee; or else three days the sword of the LORD, even the pestilence, in the land, and the angel of the LORD destroying throughout all the coasts of Israel. Now, therefore, advise thyself what word I shall bring again to him that sent me. And David said unto Gad. I am in a great strait: let me fall now into the hand of the LORD; for very great are his mercies: but let me not fall into the hand of man." 1 Chronicles 21:11-13

God allowed David to choose the judgment for his disobedience.

-   Three years of famine would be too long and too much suffering for the nation.
-   Three months of war would put Israel's enemies in control of Israel's affliction.
-   David chose the three days of pestilence, leaving the judgment to God's mercy, and God chose when to end the plaque.

"So the LORD sent a pestilence upon Israel: and there fell of Israel seventy thousand men. And God sent an angel unto Jerusalem to destroy it: and as he was destroying, the LORD beheld, and he repented him of the evil, and said to the angel that destroyed, It is enough, stay now thine hand. And the Angel of the Lord stood by the threshing floor of Ornan, the Jebusite." 1 Chronicles 21:14-16.

God stopped the plaque on the threshing floor of Ornan the Jebusite. (*a gentile*).

"Then the angel of the LORD commanded Gad to say to David, that David should go up, and set up an altar unto the LORD in the threshing floor of Ornan the Jebusite." 1 Chronicles 18.

"And as David came to Ornan, Ornan looked and saw David, and went out of the threshing floor, and bowed himself to David with his face to the ground. Then David said to Ornan, Grant me the place of this threshing floor, that I may build an altar therein unto the LORD: thou shalt grant it me for the full price: that the plague may be stayed from the people." 1 Chronicles 21:21-22.

The prophet Gad instructed David to build an altar on the place that God chose, so David built the altar on the mountain of God, Moriah.

"And Abraham called the name of that place Jehovahjireh: as it is said to this day, In the mount of the LORD it shall be seen." Genesis 22:14.

Solomon's Temple of Faith:

"Then Solomon began to build the house of the LORD at Jerusalem in mount Moriah, where the LORD appeared unto David, his father, in the place that David had prepared in the <u>threshing floor of Ornan</u> the Jebusite." 2 Chronicles 3:1.

David was not permitted by God to build the Temple because he was "a bloody man" – Warrior and Murdered. God chose the site with Abraham and Isaac, David purchased the mountain and Solomon built the Temple.

"Then said Solomon, The LORD hath said that he would dwell in the thick darkness. But I have built an house of habitation for thee, and a place for thy dwelling for ever. And the king turned his face, and blessed the whole congregation of Israel: and all the congregation of Israel stood. And he said, Blessed, be the LORD God of Israel, who hath with his hands fulfilled that which he spake with his mouth to my father David, saying, Since the day that I brought forth my people out of the land of Egypt I chose no city among all the tribes of Israel to build an house in, that my name might be there; neither chose I any man to be a ruler over my people Israel: But I have chosen Jerusalem, that my name might be there; and have chosen David to be over my people Israel. Now it was in the heart of David, my father, to build an house for the name of the LORD God of Israel. But the LORD said to David my father, Forasmuch as it was in thine heart to build an house for my name, thou didst well in that it was in thine heart: Notwithstanding thou shalt not build the house; but thy son which shall come forth out of thy loins, he shall build the house for my name. The LORD, therefore, hath performed his word that he hath spoken: for I am risen up in the room of David, my father, and am set on the throne of Israel, as the LORD promised, and have built the house for the name of the LORD God of Israel. And in it have I put the ark, wherein is the covenant of the LORD, that he made with the children of Israel. (10 Commandments)" 2 Chronicles 6:1-11.

Solomon's prayer of dedication is recorded in chapter six, and God's response is as follows.

> *"Now, when Solomon had made an end of praying, the fire came down from heaven, and consumed the burnt offering and the sacrifices; and the glory of the LORD filled the house. And the priests could not enter into the house of the LORD, because the glory of the LORD had filled the LORD'S house. And when all the children of Israel saw how the fire came down, and the glory of the LORD upon the house, they bowed themselves with their faces to the ground upon the pavement, and worshipped, and praised the LORD, saying, For he is good; for his mercy endureth forever." 2 Chronicles 7:1-3.*

God accepted Solomon's efforts in chapter seven with fire and with His Shekinah Glory moving to dwell in Solomon's Temple.

> *"And the LORD appeared to Solomon by night, and said unto him, I have heard thy prayer, and have chosen this place to myself for an house of sacrifice. If I shut up heaven that there be no rain, or if I command the locusts to devour the land, or if I send pestilence among my people; If my people, which are called by my name, shall humble themselves, and pray, and seek my face, and turn from their wicked ways; then will I hear from heaven, and will forgive their sin, and will heal their land. Now mine eyes shall be open, and mine ears attent unto the prayer that is made in this place." 2 Chronicles 12-15.*

After everything was finished and God dwelt with His people, God made a promise to Solomon and all God's believers. If my people (Israel) who are called by my name (believing Christians) will **humble** themselves, **pray, seek** God, and **turn** from their wickedness, God will **Hear**, **Forgive**, and **Heal** their land.

We need to be seeking God's forgiveness and be asking Him to heal America because of the consequences of turning away from God are as recorded by Hosea.

> *"My people are destroyed for lack of knowledge: because thou hast rejected knowledge, I will also reject thee, that thou shalt be no priest to me: <u>seeing thou hast forgotten the law of thy God, I will also forget thy children.</u>" Hosea 4:6.*

<u>Moriah, the Mountain of Faith:</u>

Abraham's sacrifice of his beloved son is an example of God's sacrifice of His son Jesus for our sins.

> *"That whosoever believeth in him should not perish, but have eternal life. For God so loved the world, that he gave his <u>only begotten Son,</u> that whosoever believeth in him should not perish, but have everlasting life. For God sent not his Son into the world to condemn the world; but that the world through him might be saved. He that believeth on him is not condemned: but he that believeth not is condemned already because he hath not believed in the name of the only begotten Son of God." John 3:15-18.*

It doesn't get any clearer than that. Faith in Jesus equals eternal life. Forgiveness of sin is through the sacrifice of Jesus. Ask, and your sins shall will be forgiven, and your eternal life obtained.

> *"And the Word (Jesus) was made flesh, and dwelt among us, (and we beheld his glory, the glory as of the only begotten of the Father,) full of grace and truth." John 1:14.*

Jesus, enclosing the Shekinah Glory of God, entered Solomon's Temple in Matthew twenty-three.

> *"And after six days Jesus taketh Peter, James, and John, his brother, and bringeth them up into an high mountain apart, And was transfigured before them: and his face did shine as the sun, and his raiment was white as the light. And, behold, there appeared unto them Moses and Elias talking with him. Then answered Peter, and said unto Jesus, Lord, it is good for us to be here: if thou wilt, let us make here three tabernacles; one for thee, and one for Moses, and one for Elias. While he yet spake, behold, a bright cloud overshadowed them: and behold a voice out of the cloud, which said, This is my beloved Son, in whom I am well pleased; hear ye him. And when the disciples heard it, they fell on their face, and were sore afraid. And Jesus came and touched them, and said, Arise, and be not afraid. And when they had lifted up their eyes, they saw no man, save Jesus only." Matthew 17:1-8.*

Peter wanted to build dwelling places for Moses, Elijah, and Jesus. God responded, *"This is my beloved Son, in whom I am well pleased; hear ye him."*

"And Abraham called the name of that place Jehovahjireh as it is said to this day, In the mount of the LORD: (the Temple Mount) it shall be seen." Genesis 22:14.

God's chosen Millennial Temple site:

On top of this mountain will be the New Jerusalem and the Millennial Temple. The prophet Isaiah speaks of this.

"And it shall come to pass in the last days, that the mountain of the LORD'S house shall be established in the top of the mountains, and shall be exalted above the hills; and all nations shall flow unto it. And many people shall go and say, Come ye, and let us go up to the mountain of the LORD, to the house of the God of Jacob; and he will teach us of his ways, and we will walk in his paths: for out of Zion shall go forth the law and the word of the LORD from Jerusalem. And he shall judge among the nations, and shall rebuke many people: and they shall beat their swords into plowshares, and their spears into pruninghooks: nation shall not lift up sword against nation, neither shall they learn war any more." Isaiah 2:2-4.

The passage clearly states that this mountain will be the highest of all mountains on the globe because it is most exalted and holy. All the nations will come to the mountain of God to learn the ways of Jehovah because the law of the millennium will emanate from this mountain. The Temple on the mountain will also become the center of Jewish worship and a place of prayer for all nations.

"And it shall come to pass in that day, that the great trumpet shall be blown, and they shall come which were ready to perish in the land of Assyria, and the outcasts in the land of Egypt, and shall worship the LORD in the holy mount at Jerusalem." Isaiah 27:13

"Also the sons of the stranger, that join themselves to the LORD, to serve Him, and to love the name of the LORD, to be his servants, every one that keepeth the sabbath from polluting it, and taketh hold of my covenant; Even them will I bring to my holy mountain, and make them joyful in my house of prayer: their burnt offerings and their sacrifices shall be accepted upon mine altar; for mine, house shall be called an house of prayer for all people. The Lord GOD which gathereth the outcasts of Israel saith, Yet will I gather others to him, beside those that are gathered unto him." Isaiah 56:6-8.

Ezekiel states that the total size of the mountain of Jehovah's house is to be 50 miles wide and fifty miles deep. It will be the holy oblation upon which both the Millennial Temple and the City of Jerusalem will sit.

"All the oblation shall be five and twenty thousand by five and twenty thousand: ye shall offer the holy oblation foursquare, with the possession of the city." Ezekiel 48:20.

Ezekiel, at the end of his prophecy, gives details on the size of the city of God. All four sides will be fifty miles long with three gates each. The gates are named for each of the twelve tribes of

Israel. Jerusalem will be renamed. Jerusalem (the city of peace) will be called **Jehovah Shammah** (Jehovah is there).

> *"And these are the goings out of the city on the north side, four thousand and five hundred measures. And the gates of the city shall be after the names of the tribes of Israel: three gates northward; one gate of Reuben, one gate of Judah, one gate of Levi. And at the east side four thousand and five hundred: and three gates; and one gate of Joseph, one gate of Benjamin, one gate of Dan. And at the south side four thousand and five hundred measures: and three gates; one gate of Simeon, one gate of Issachar, one gate of Zebulun. At the west side four thousand and five hundred, with their three gates; one gate of Gad, one gate of Asher, one gate of Naphtali. It was round about eighteen thousand measures: and the name of the city from that day shall be, The LORD is there." Ezekiel 48:30-35.*

The Talmud describes the dazzling beauty of the New Jerusalem as *"Ten parts of beauty were allotted to the world at large, out of these Jerusalem assumed nine and the rest of the world but one."* Scripture also indicates that the New Jerusalem will be raised higher, probably during the tribulation earthquake.

This area will include a 20-mile by 50-mile area for the Temple, living areas for the priests, and the sons of Zadock. The tribe of Levi will have a 20-mile by 50-mile area, and there will be two food growing areas 10-mile by 20-mile with a 10-mile by 10-mile area between them for the New Jerusalem.

God elaborates on the promise made through Zechariah 1:14-17 in the second chapter of Zechariah's prophecy with the vision of a man with a measuring line. The man is identified in the text as

Malakh Jehovah. The Angel of Jehovah, the Second person of the Trinity, Jesus incarnate. God will choose and rebuild Jerusalem greater than before. It will be inhabited as a city without defenses, as God will be the builder and protector of the New World capital. The city will be significantly enlarged, extending much beyond the boundaries of the ancient walls. People will inhabit the plains or open country surrounding the new city with suburbs.

Physical walls around Jerusalem will not be for security but beauty. In addition to Jehovah's dwelling there, the Shekinah Glory of God will surround the city in the form of fire (v. 5). The glory of the Lord shall lighten it, and the lamb shall be the lamp thereof (v23). God, in the person Messiah Jesus will dwell in Jerusalem and from his throne will reign over Israel and the entire world.

> *"Therefore they shall come and sing in the height of Zion..." Jeremiah 31:12*

Jerusalem will also become a Riverside city.

> *"And his feet shall stand in that day upon the Mount of Olives, which is before Jerusalem on the east, and the mount of Olives shall cleave in the midst thereof toward the east and toward the west, and there shall be a very great valley; and half of the mountain shall remove toward the north and half of it toward the south. And ye shall flee to the valley of the mountains; for the valley of the mountains shall reach unto Azal: yea, ye shall flee, like as ye fled from before the earthquake in the days of Uzziah king of Judah: and the LORD my God shall come, and all the saints with thee. And it shall come to pass in that day, that the light shall not be clear, nor dark: But it shall be one day which shall be known to*

the LORD, not day, nor night: but it shall come to pass, that at evening time it shall be light. And it shall be in that day, that living waters shall go out from Jerusalem; half of them toward the former sea, and half of them toward the hinder sea:.." Zechariah 14:4-8.

Prof. (Dr.) WA. Liebenberg explains how God has arranged the topography to provide a freshwater stream out of the temple that will heal the land of Israel and the salt sea.

HaShem Digs a River Bed:

"Afterward, he brought me again unto the door of the house; and, behold, waters issued out from under the threshold of the house eastward: for the forefront of the house stood toward the east, and the waters came down from under from the right side of the house, at the south side of the altar. Then brought he me out of the way of the gate northward, and led me about the way without unto the utter gate by the way that looketh eastward; and, behold, there ran out waters on the right side. And when the man that had the line in his hand went forth eastward, he measured a thousand cubits, and he brought me through the waters; the waters were to the ankles. Again he measured a thousand, and brought me through the waters; the waters were to the knees. Again he measured a thousand, and brought me through; the waters were to the loins. Afterward, he measured a thousand; and it was a river that I could not pass over: for the waters were risen,

*waters to swim in, a river that could not be
passed over." Ezekiel 47:2-5.*

*"As is typical of springs that surface from karst topography, when one
precedes eastward from the spring source, he or she notes that it becomes
wider and deeper. Like many other springs, and waters that flow away
from its source cut a V-shaped Valley through the limestone strata it will
eventually be fed by side springs from the limestone water table among
the lower sections of the V. This feeding by subterranean springs from the
water table will eventually cause the millennial stream becomes wider
and deeper as one proceeds eastward from its temple spring source. As
you may observe, the actual cubic measure begins at the "utter gate" of
the newly built millennial Temple. The measurements of 4000 cubits,
or 6000 feet, carries us directly through the valley created by HaShem
between the remaining halves of Mount of Olives and on the opposite
side of where the Mount of Olives once stood, a sudden hydrological
change occurs at the end of the measurement. The increase in depth the
spring stream is very gradual for the first 4000 cubits, going from the
ankles to the knees to the thighs. But suddenly, at the end of the 4000
cubits, Ezekiel encounters a river that he cannot pass through except my
swimming. It is very possible that this great river is the diverted Jordan
River."* Prof. (Dr.) WA. Liebenberg,

God will dwell in the midst of Jerusalem:

The first eight verses of Zechariah chapter eight describe the
Millennial Jerusalem.

*"Again the word of the LORD of hosts came to
me, saying, Thus saith the LORD of hosts; I was
jealous for Zion with great jealousy, and I was
jealous for her with great fury. Thus saith the
LORD; I am returned unto Zion, and will dwell*

in the midst of Jerusalem: and Jerusalem shall be called a city of truth; and the mountain of the LORD of hosts the holy mountain. Thus saith the LORD of hosts; There shall yet old men and old women dwell in the streets of Jerusalem, and every man with his staff in his hand for very age. And the streets of the city shall be full of boys and girls playing in the streets thereof. Thus saith the LORD of hosts; If it be marvellous in the eyes of the remnant of this people in these days, should it also be marvellous in mine eyes? saith the LORD of hosts. Thus saith the LORD of hosts; Behold, I will save my people from the east country, and from the west country; And I will bring them, and they shall dwell in the midst of Jerusalem: and they shall be my people, and I will be their God, in truth and in righteousness." Zechariah 8:1-8.

God's special love for Jerusalem will cause Him to dwell in her midst, just as He did in Solomon's day. Jerusalem will become the city of truth upon the mountain of Jehovah's house. The city will be inhabited by all ages, from the very young, those who will be born in the kingdom, to the very old some living well into their hundreds of years. The millennial Jerusalem will be the most beautiful city in the entire world and will be inhabited by Jews regathered from the nations all around the world.

5

New World Population

"There shall be no more thence an infant of days, nor an old man that hath not filled his days: for the child shall die an hundred years old; but the sinner being an hundred years old shall be accursed," Isaiah 65: 20

With this present world virtually destroyed by God's judgment of the Antichrist and his followers in the seven-year tribulation period, who will be the inhabitants of God's New World and his capital, **Jehovah Shammah?** Many classifications of people will make up the population of the Millennial Kingdom.

The Raptured Believers:

The first group will be those who return with Christ at the end of the Campaign of Armageddon. These are the saints that were caught up to be with Christ at the time of the Rapture. John recorded Jesus' explanation of this event:

> *"Let not your heart be troubled: ye believe in God, believe also in me. In my Father's house are many mansions: if it were not so, I would have told you. I go to prepare a place for you. And if I go and prepare a place for you, I will come again, and receive you unto myself; that where I am, there ye may be also." John 14:1-3.*

Jesus, about 2000 years ago, made this promise of his return to his disciples. Jesus told them he was going back to heaven to prepare magnificent dwelling places for his followers and that someday he would return to take them to dwell with him in heaven. This passage speaks of what is referred to as the Rapture, where Jesus returns in the clouds of the air and calls his believers up to him and then leads them back to heaven. At the same time, he judges an unbelieving, rebellious world during the tribulation period on the earth.

The apostle Paul answering a question the believers had raised in Thessalonica about what will happen to their believing friends who have died and missed out on the benefits of the rapture said:

> *"But I would not have you to be ignorant, brethren, concerning them which are asleep, that ye sorrow not, even as others which have no hope. For if we believe that Jesus died and rose again, even so, them also which sleep in Jesus will God bring with him. For this, we say unto you by the word of the Lord, that we which are alive and remain unto the coming of the Lord shall not prevent them which are asleep. For the Lord, himself shall descend from heaven with a shout, with the voice of the archangel, and with the*

> *trump of God: and the dead in Christ shall rise*
> *first: Then we which are alive and remain shall*
> *be caught up together with them in the clouds, to*
> *meet the Lord in the air: and so shall we ever be*
> *with the Lord. Wherefore comfort one another*
> *with these words." 1 Thessalonians 4:13-18.*

The believers in Thessalonica believed that the Lord would return for them but did not understand God also included the resurrection of the saints who had died. Paul even comforts them by letting them know that the believers who had died receive the benefits of the Rapture first. Paul uses the term 'sleep' to indicate that these saints are only having a temporary suspension of earthly activity until one awakens, yet there is no suspension of mental activity. He is not talking about soul sleep because the Bible says that the soul will be *absent from the body and present the Lord.* Then he reveals the chronological sequence of the rapture event in its seven stages.

First: *the Lord himself will descend from heaven.* Jesus will descend into Earth's atmosphere from heaven.

Second: *with a shout.* The chief commander, Jesus, will shout for the resurrection and translation to occur.

Third: *with the voice of the archangel.* Michael, the archangel, will set the rapture into motion, as he repeats the command.

Fourth: *with the trump of God.* The sound of the Shofar serves as a summons to put the plan into motion.

Fifth: *the dead in Christ shall rise first.* This is the resurrection of the deceased believers who had died before the Rapture. This resurrection is for the New Testament Church saints only.

Sixth: *Then we which are alive and remain shall be caught up together with them in the clouds,* refers to the translation of the living saints. The living believers will be caught up with the deceased saints and be united with the Lord Jesus Christ in the heavens.

Seventh: *to meet the Lord in the air:* the final step is the fact that both the resurrected believers, and the glorified living believers will both join the Messiah in the air.

The apostle Paul deals with the change in our earthly bodies in his letter to the Corinthians.

> *"Now this I say, brethren, that flesh and blood cannot inherit the kingdom of God; neither doth corruption inherit incur-ruption. Behold, I show you a mystery; We shall not all sleep, but we shall all be changed, In a moment, in the twinkling of an eye, at the last trump: for the trumpet shall sound, and the dead shall be raised incorruptible, and we shall be changed. For this corruptible must put on incorruption, and this mortal must put on immortality. So when this corruptible shall have put on incorruption, and this mortal shall have put on immortality, then shall be brought to pass the saying that is written, Death is swallowed up in victory. O death, where is thy sting? O grave, where is thy victory? The sting of death is sin; and the strength of sin is the law. But thanks be to God, which giveth us the victory through our Lord Jesus Christ. Therefore, my beloved brethren, be ye stedfast, unmoveable, always abounding in the work of the Lord, forasmuch as ye know that your labour is not in vain in the Lord." 1 Corinthians 15:50-58.*

Because of sin, man has become subject to corruption and mortality.

> *"Wherefore, as by one man sin entered into the world, and death by sin; and so death passed upon all men, for that all have sinned: For*

until the law sin was in the world: but sin is not imputed when there is no law. Nevertheless, death reigned from Adam to Moses, even over them that had not sinned after the similitude of Adam's transgression, who is the figure of him that was to come." Romans 5:12-14.

Our physical bodies are subject to corruption and mortality because we have inherited the sinful nature of our ancestors, since the time of Adam and Eve. Before our bodies can enter eternity, God must change us into glorified bodies like Jesus.

"When the believer's clock strikes rapture, look out! A real fountain of youth will appear, at last! We ourselves groan within ourselves, waiting for the adoption, to wit, the redemption of our body (Romans 8:23). Our fountain of youth will prove to be a translation from mortality to immortality, through Jesus. Live reality will soon transcend old theology!" George Otis Sr.

Paul describes this change from earthly bodies to heavenly bodies.

"Behold, I show you a mystery; We shall not all sleep, but we shall all be changed, In a moment, in the twinkling of an eye, at the last trump: for the trumpet shall sound, and the dead shall be raised incorruptible, and we shall be changed. For this corruptible must put on incorruption, and this mortal must put on immortality." 1 Corinthians 15:51-53.

Our physical bodies must be changed to a new body to function in God's heaven.

First, it is a body that is incorruptible.

Second, it is a glorified body.

Third, it is a body of resurrection power.

Fourth, it is a spiritual body.

Fifth, it is a heavenly body.

Sixth, it is an immortal body.

This change will take place very rapidly, *in the twinkling of an eye as defined. "A slight, intermittent gleam of light; a sparkling flash; a glimmer."* The free dictionary.

This event known as the Rapture is when Messiah Jesus comes back in the clouds of the air and calls his church saints to be caught up in the air with him and takes us all back to heaven with him to live in glorified bodies until the judgments of the Tribulation period are completed. We will then return with him to rule over all the nations of the earth for a thousand years.

> *"And I saw heaven opened and behold a white horse; and he that sat upon him was called Faithful and True, and in righteousness he doth judge and make war. His eyes were as a flame of fire, and on his head were many crowns; and he had a name written, that no man knew, but he himself. And he was clothed with a vesture dipped in blood: and his name is called The Word of God. And the armies which were in heaven followed him upon white horses, clothed in fine linen, white and clean." Revelation 19:11-14.*

Tribulation Survivors:

With billions dead after the Tribulation, some people may survive and enter Jesus' New World Order in their human bodies.
"But he that shall endure unto the end, the same shall be saved." Matthew24:13.

All disasters have a few survivors. There may be millions who have survived Satan's rule, as more than half the world population will have died in the twenty-one judgments and the Campaign of Armageddon. These natural human beings will live all around the world during this time.

Human Beings have always survived various natural and manmade disasters. People survive car accidents, floods, tidal waves, hurricanes, tornadoes, and all kinds of things. Incidents that should kill them, yet somehow, they escaped death even though they may be injured.

And also, those who are in their natural human bodies during that time will have their chance to be converted and become children of God in the Kingdom of God!

During the Millennium, non-glorified people will experience longevity similar to those who lived before the Genesis flood. Jesus will be present on earth, Satan will be out of business, and God will allow no wicked people to corrupt society. However, in the millennium, mortals who don't accept the saving grace of Jesus will die because death will still remain. Since God is always giving humankind a choice between good and evil, people still need to accept Jesus for salvation. Also, the children born during the Millennium will have to choose for themselves to follow Christ or reject Him.

In Moses day, God challenged all people:

"See, I have set before thee this day life and good, and death and evil;" Deuteronomy 30:15

This choice of life or death has been going on since the beginning. Until they were tested, Adam and Eve were denied access to the incredible tree of life. With an assist from the serpent, they blew it and were ejected from Eden lest they eat of that eternal-life tree. God knew that as a consequence of the fall, they would grow more and more evil. Thus God dare not permit them to live forever. Otherwise through the centuries they would have developed into grotesque, reprobate beings. George Otis.

> **"He that hath an ear, let him hear what the Spirit saith unto the churches; To him that overcometh will I give to eat of the tree of life, which is in the midst of the paradise of God." Revelation 2:7.**

When we're raptured, every physical flaw and weakness will be gone. God erases all our imperfections resulting from sin, environment, and heredity. At that time we will become what God originally intended.

> **"Who shall change our vile body, that it may be fashioned like unto his glorious body, according to the working whereby he is able even to subdue all things unto himself." Philippians 3:21.**

Each of the millennial saints will be perfect and strikingly beautiful! At some microsecond, glorified saints will find themselves better than in their prime years, pulsing with beauty, vitality, and freshness.

"The built-in capacity of the human body to replace its own cells may hint and millennium's eternal youth capability. Most cells of our body can replace themselves when damaged or worn out. It seems reasonable that this automatic cellular replacement will be perfected in the millennium, so a thousand-year-old man could easily retain the glow of youth. There would be a continual renewing of our every cell." George Otis.

Resurrected New Testament Saints:

> *"Thy dead men shall live, together with my dead body shall they arise. Awake and sing, ye that dwell in dust: for thy dew is as the dew of herbs, and the earth shall cast out the dead."* Isaiah 26:19.

> *"And many of them that sleep in the dust of the earth shall awake, some to everlasting life, and some to shame and everlasting contempt."* Daniel 12:2.

These verses show that the Rapture before the Great Tribulation will only include the Church saints. God will resurrect the Old Testament saints as part of the events of the first 75 days of the Messiah's return and the establishment of His earthly rule.

"A more literal rendering of Daniel 12:2 would read as follows: and [at that time] many [of your people] shall awake or be separated out from among the sleepers in the Earth's dust. These will wake unto life everlasting, but those [rest of the sleepers who do not awake at this time] shall be unto shame and contempt everlasting." Dr. Arnold Fruchtenbaum.

This reveals the difference between the resurrection of the righteous and the resurrection of the unrighteous. Only the righteous will be resurrected at this time to take part in the blessings of the Millennial Kingdom. These are the friends of the bridegroom who are invited to the wedding feast with which the Millennium will begin.

Jim Zeigler

The Tribulation Martyrs:

Besides the resurrection of the Old Testament saints, there also is the resurrection of those saints who were martyred in the course of the Great Tribulation.

> *"And I saw thrones, and they sat upon them, and judgment was given unto them: and I saw the souls of them that were beheaded for the witness of Jesus, and for the word of God, and which had not worshipped the beast, neither his image, neither had received his mark upon their foreheads, or in their hands; and they lived and reigned with Christ a thousand years."* **Revelation 20:4.**

In this passage, John the Revelator sees the second group of people ruling with the Messiah. These are the saints who have been beheaded because they did not worship the Antichrist or his image, or receive the mark of the beast. These are the tribulation saints that will be resurrected at this time.

With the resurrection of the tribulation saints, the first resurrection is completed. The second resurrection will take place 1,000 years later. According to verse six, the first resurrection involves only believes, and that is why *"the one who waits for and reaches the end of the 1,335 days."* is blessed to be a participant in the first resurrection. The first resurrection comes in stages in an orderly progression.

> *"But now is Christ risen from the dead, and become the firstfruits of them that slept. For since by man came death, by man came also the resurrection of the dead. For as in Adam all die, even so in Christ shall all be made alive. But*

every man in his own order: Christ the firstfruits; afterward they that are Christ's at his coming." 1 Corinthians 15:20-23.

Paul declares that the righteous will be resurrected *in his own order.* The word translated order is a military term used for the sequence of troops marching in position. God will not resurrect all the righteous at the same time but in sequential order. The first resurrection includes five stages:

First - the resurrection of Jesus.

Second - the resurrection of the Church saints, the Rapture.

Third - the resurrection of the Two Witnesses in the middle of the tribulation.

Forth - the resurrection of the Old Testament saints during the 75-day interval.

Fifth -the resurrection of the Tribulation saints.

"When the kingdom begins, all-natural men, both Jews, and Gentiles, will be believers. The Jews in their entirety will be saved just prior to the Second Coming of the Messiah. All unbelieving Gentiles, goats, will be killed during the 75-year interval between the Tribulation and the Millennium, and only believing Gentiles, sheep, be able to enter the kingdom." Dr. Arnold Fruchtenbaum.

6

New World Worship

"Yea, many people, and strong nations shall come to seek the LORD of hosts in Jerusalem and to pray before the LORD. Thus saith the LORD of hosts; In those days it shall come to pass, that ten men shall take hold out of all languages of the nations, even shall take hold of the skirt of him that is a Jew, saying, We will go with you: for we have heard that God is with you."
Ezekiel 8:22-23.

The New Temple of Worship:

Ezekiel 40:5 through 43:27 describes the eight sections of the Millennial Temple area.

The first section concerns the outer court. Ezekiel describes the outer court, the Eastern Gate, the thirty chambers in the pavement around the outer court, the northern gate in the southern gate. A 'cubit' is equal to about 20.5 inches, and a 'reed' is approximately six cubits (10 foot, 3 inches).

"And behold a wall on the outside of the house round about, and in the man's hand a measuring reed of six cubits long by the cubit and an hand breadth: so he measured the breadth of the building, one reed; and the height, one reed. Then came he unto the gate which looketh toward the east, and went up the stairs thereof, and measured the threshold of the gate, which was one reed broad; and the other threshold of the gate, which was one reed broad. And every little chamber was one reed long, and one reed broad; and between the little chambers were five cubits; and the threshold of the gate by the porch of the gate within was one reed. He measured also the porch of the gate within, one reed. Then measured he the porch of the gate, eight cubits; and the posts thereof, two cubits; and the porch of the gate was inward. And the little chambers of the gate eastward were three on this side, and three on that side; they three were of one measure: and the posts had one measure on this side and on that side. And he measured the breadth of the entry of the gate, ten cubits; and the length of the gate, thirteen cubits. The space also before the little chambers was one cubit on this side, and the space was one cubit on that side: and the little chambers were six cubits on this side, and six cubits on that side. He measured then the gate from the roof of one little chamber to the roof of another: the breadth was five and twenty

cubits, door against door. He made also posts of threescore cubits, even unto the post of the court round about the gate. And from the face of the gate of the entrance unto the face of the porch of the inner gate were fifty cubits. And there were narrow windows to the little chambers, and to their posts within the gate round about, and likewise to the arches: and windows were round about inward: and upon each post were palm trees. Then brought he me into the outward court, and, lo, there were chambers, and a pavement made for the court round about: thirty chambers were upon the pavement. And the pavement by the side of the gates over against the length of the gates was the lower pavement. Then he measured the breadth from the forefront of the lower gate unto the forefront of the inner court without, an hundred cubits eastward and northward. And the gate of the outward court that looked toward the north, he measured the length thereof, and the breadth thereof. And the little chambers thereof were three on this side and three on that side; and the posts thereof and the arches thereof were after the measure of the first gate: the length thereof was fifty cubits, and the breadth five and twenty cubits. And their windows, and their arches, and their palm trees, were after the measure of the gate that looketh toward the east; and they went up unto it by seven steps; and the arches thereof were before them. And the gate of the inner court was over against the gate toward the north, and toward the east; and he measured from gate to gate an hundred cubits. After that, he brought me toward the south, and behold a gate toward the south: and he measured the posts thereof and the arches thereof according to these measures. And there were windows in it and in the arches thereof round about, like those windows: the length was fifty cubits, and the breadth five and twenty cubits. And there were seven steps to go up to it, and the arches thereof were before them: and it had palm trees, one on this side, and another on that side, upon the posts thereof. And there was a gate in the inner court toward the south: and he measured from gate to gate toward the south an hundred cubits." Ezekiel 40:5-27.

The second section describes the inner court. Here Ezekiel describes four things. First, the gates of the inner court, composed of the Southern gate area, the Eastern gate area in the Northern gate area; next, he describes the table for preparing the sacrifices; and the chambers for the ministering priests; and finally, the Altar for Millennial Sacrifice. (Ezekiel 40:28-47).

The third section describes the Millennial Temple itself, including the porch, the posts, the Holy Place with its entrance, the Holy of Holies, the Temple wall and chambers, the separate area, the interior of the Temple, and the exterior of the Temple. (Ezekiel 40:48-41:26)

The fourth section describes the chambers of the outer court. (Ezekiel 42:1-14)

The fifth section describes the outer wall. (Ezekiel 42:15-20)

The sixth section records the return of the Shekinah Glory. The Shekinah Glory authenticated and sanctioned Solomon's Temple. This will confirm the promise that the Shekinah Glory will never depart from Israel again, but dwell amidst Israel forever. (Ezekiel 43:1-9)

The seventh section is a command to the prophet Ezekiel to point out the sinfulness of Israel considering the coming Holy

Oblation, and how much more shall Israel be ashamed of their present sinfulness. (Ezekiel 43:1-12)

The eighth section is a description of the altar. It includes the measurement of the altar and the consecration of the altar. (Ezekiel 43:13-27)

This is the Millennial Temple that is to be the center of Jewish and Gentile worship during the Millennium. Later, Ezekiel described God's sanctuary.

> *"Moreover I will make a covenant of peace with them; it shall be an everlasting covenant with them: and I will place them, and multiply them, and will set my sanctuary in the midst of them for evermore. My tabernacle also shall be with them: yea, I will be their God, and they shall be my people. And the heathen shall know that I the LORD do sanctify Israel, when my sanctuary shall be in the midst of them for evermore."*
> *Ezekiel 37:26-28*

"Since God himself in the person of the Messiah (Jesus) will be dwelling in and reigning from Jerusalem, there will be no need of any Ark of the Covenant. Furthermore, the Ark of the Covenant contained the tablets of stone that were the embodiment of the Law of Moses. The fact that the Law of Moses is no longer in effect is a reason why the Ark of the Covenant will be missing.

There will be a sacrificial system instituted in the millennium that will have some features similar to the Mosaic system, along with some brand-new laws. For that very reason, the sacrificial system of the Millennium must not be viewed as a reinstitution of the Mosaic system because it is not. It will be a brand-new system that will continue some things old and something's new and will be instituted for an entirely different purpose." Dr. Arnold G. Fruchtenbaum.

In Old Testament times, the sacrificial offerings brought into the temple provided food and other specialties for the priests and Levites. They were bound to certain portions of meat and grain offerings themselves. Since they had no inheritance for themselves, God dispersed the priesthood throughout the nation, and for caring for the tribes, they served as religious leaders.

"Jacob's prophecy that Levi's descendants would be scattered throughout Israel (Genesis 49:7) was fulfilled when God appointed them as the priestly tribe who, unlike the other tribes, would receive no land inheritance. However, in God's sovereign and mysterious way, Jacob's prophecy turned into a blessing because Levi's inheritance was better than land—it was God Himself (Numbers 18:20). And God promised to provide for the Levites from the abundance of all of the other tribes (Numbers 18:8–14)." www.gotquestions.org.

The offerings in the Millennium will provide for the Temple priests, administration, and maintenance of the Temple.

The sacrifices in the Millennium Temple will not be a picture pointing to the sacrifice of Christ for our salvation, but will be a demonstration of our love and devotion to God. The privilege of life and physical blessings in the theocratic kingdom will be contingent upon outward conformity to the ceremonial law. Such compliance will not bring salvation. But a legalistic system of enforced participation will uphold their symbolic value. For example, drought or plague will punish those who decide not to take part in the annual feast of Tabernacles.

The sacrifice of Christ is the only acceptable remedy for sin. The Old Testament sacrifices looked forward to this, but they could not take away sin. Millennium sacrifices have no efficacious value and cannot take away sin either. God ordained the Old Testament sacrifices in anticipation of the death of Christ. The millennial sacrifices will be a reminder of the sacrifice of Christ, much like the Lord's supper is a reminder of his death on the cross to us today.

In the ideal situation of the millennial kingdom, sin will not take on the ugly characteristics that it now has, and some people would question why Christ had to die. Sacrifices, and the scars on His hands and feet, are a reminder of His sacrifice for our forgiveness.

There will be two feasts observed during the Millennium: Passover and the Feast of Tabernacles. The Jewish people will teach the meaning of these fees to the Gentiles. The word *feast* in Hebrew means *a set for an appointed time.*

"Remember this truth: everything God will do; he has already done. Gentile believers will need a teacher, and the Jewish people will be delighted to share the Jewish roots of Christianity as found in God's Word." John Hagee.

Spiritual Life in the Kingdom is one of joy, peace, righteousness, and worship. Because the rule of the Messiah is perfect, it also affects the other aspects of life on earth. The curse that was brought on earth by Adam's sin is lifted, as revealed in Isaiah 35:1-2, which speaks of the abundance and fertility of the soil:

> *"The wilderness and the solitary place shall be glad for them, and the desert shall rejoice, and blossom as the rose. It shall blossom abundantly, and rejoice even with joy and singing: the glory of Lebanon shall be given unto it, the excellency of Carmel and Sharon, they shall see the glory of the LORD, and the excellency of our God." Isiah 35:1-2.*

At the end of the Millennium, many will still rebel and follow Satan, who was released *"for a short season."* As children are born and grow up, they, too, will have to make spiritual decisions. They can go through the motions of following Christ without really believing; thus, some of them will rebel against God at the end of the Millennium.

Jim Zeigler

Law of Moses ended:

> *"Seventy weeks are determined upon thy people and upon thy holy city, to finish the transgression, and to make an end of sins, and to make reconciliation for iniquity, and to bring in everlasting righteousness, and to seal up the vision and prophecy, and to anoint the most Holy. Know therefore and understand, that from the going forth of the commandment to restore and to build Jerusalem unto the Messiah the Prince shall be seven weeks, and threescore and two weeks: the street shall be built again, and the wall, even in troublous times. And after threescore and two weeks shall Messiah be cut off, but not for himself: and the people of the prince that shall come shall destroy the city and the sanctuary; and the end thereof shall be with a flood, and unto the end of the war desolations are determined. And he shall confirm the covenant with many for one week: and in the midst of the week he shall cause the sacrifice and the oblation to cease. For the overspreading of abominations, he shall make it desolate, even until the consummation, and that determined shall be poured upon the desolate."*
> *Daniel 9:24-27.*

Daniel, the prophet who lived 2500 years ago, foretold of the future of his nation, Israel, and God's dealings with them through the law of Moses. (Leviticus 26:27-34) He gave the detailed timing of when the Messiah would come. Daniel's prophecy covered a period of 70 weeks or 70 periods of seven years (490 years). The first 483 years (69 weeks of seven years) started with the decree issued by Babylonian King Cyrus to rebuild Jerusalem and ended with the coming of the Messiah Jesus entering the city of Jerusalem on Palm Sunday.

However, what Daniel could not see was the last week of seven years were separated by the period known as the Church Age because the Jews rejected Jesus as Messiah. The Church age will end with the Rapture of the Church. We live in that age now, also known as the Age of Grace. Current history and events happening now are pointing to the end of this Age of Grace when Christ returns to take His church to heaven bodily to be with him. See my first book ***Look Up: Redemption in this Generation,*** for the signs leading to Jesus Rapture of His church.

> *"In my Father's house are many mansions: if it were not so, I would have told you. I go to prepare a place for you. And if I go and prepare a place for you, I will come again, and receive you unto myself; that where I am, there ye may be also."* ***John 12:2-3.***

The last week of Daniel's prophecy will happen after the Church is removed. I wrote about this time in my book ***Look Out: the World without Christians.*** You don't want to live through this. Over half the world population will perish from the seven seal judgments, seven trumpet judgments, seven vial judgments, and the three woes pronounced by Almighty God to judge the followers of the Antichrist. The end of the Tribulation will mark the end of Daniel's prophecies and the end of the Mosaic law.

The Millennial Priesthood and Sacrifices:

Three chapters in the book of Ezekiel are concerned with the various laws regulating the millennial system of priesthood and sacrifice. Though similar to the commandments of the law of

Moses, there are some significant differences. During the messianic kingdom, a whole new system of kingdom law will govern. The significant sections dealing with the millennial laws are recorded in Ezekiel 44:1 to 46:24.

The first section concerns the law of the outer Eastern gate. Ezekiel states that at the beginning of the Millennium Kingdom, this gate will be shut, never to be reopened again for a thousand years.

> *"Then he brought me back the way of the gate of the outward sanctuary which looketh toward the east; and it was shut. Then said the LORD unto me; This gate shall be shut, it shall not be opened, and no man shall enter in by it; because the LORD, the God of Israel, hath entered in by it, therefore it shall be shut. It is for the prince; the prince, he shall sit in it to eat bread before the LORD; he shall enter by the way of the porch of that gate, and shall go out by the way of the same." Ezekiel 44:1-3.*

God will lock it because the Shekinah Glory returned through this gate never to depart from Israel again.

The present Eastern or Golden Gate is called by the Arabs, Bab-ad-Daharia, *'the occasional gate'* because, in ancient times, it was only opened on rare occasions, such as for the king or the anointing of a new High Priest.

Because of the prophecies of the Messiah's return through this gate, it was sealed centuries ago by the Ottoman Turks. To further hinder the Jewish Messiah, the Arab's built a Moslem cemetery right up to the very walls of the Gate, reasoning that Messiah would not defile Himself by passing through a burial ground.

In the last century, there have been two attempts to re-open the Eastern Gate. Both were stopped by war. In 1917, the Muslims attempted to open the gate, and the same day Jerusalem passed out of Muslin control into the hands of the British. The Turks fled British General Allenby. He had dropped leaflets warning the Muslim citizens of the coming attached and signed them General Allenby. However, the Turks interpreted it as a sign from Allah, not Allenby.

Fifty years later, in 1967, a Muslin controlled Jerusalem government was about to open the sealed Eastern Gate, to construct a new hotel when the workmen were forced to flee as the Israeli army took Jerusalem in the "Six Days War." Wars halted two attempts to open the gate on the same day that the workers were to open the sealed Eastern Gate.

The Prince, David, was resurrected along with the Old Testament Saints when Jesus rose from the dead, and he eat before the gate, but his entrance was through the porch only. Since the gate is permanently sealed, entry and exit can only be from the porch.

"It should be pointed out that this passage of Scripture has nothing to do with the present Eastern gate of Jerusalem, known today as the Golden gate. This passage, in its context, is not dealing with the Jerusalem today but is dealing with the temple gate in the millennium. The gate of Jesus's day was destroyed in A.D. 70. The present Golden gate was built in the seventh century and later modified by the Crusaders. It was partially destroyed by the Ottoman Turks and rebuilt in the early 16th century. It was walled up by the Turkish governor of Jerusalem in 1530." Dr. Arnold Fruchtenbaum.

The second section of Ezekiel's prophecy contains another message of the Shekinah glory, which again points to Israel's present sins.

"Then brought he me the way of the north gate before the house: and I looked, and, behold, the glory of the LORD filled the house of the LORD: and I fell upon my face. And the LORD said unto me, Son of man, mark well, and behold with

thine eyes, and hear with thine ears all that I say unto thee concerning all the ordinances of the house of the LORD, and all the laws thereof; and mark well the entering in of the house, with every going forth of the sanctuary. And thou shalt say to the rebellious, even to the house of Israel, Thus saith the Lord GOD; O ye house of Israel, let it suffice you of all your abominations, In that ye have brought into my sanctuary strangers, uncircumcised in heart, and uncircumcised in flesh, to be in my sanctuary, to pollute it, even my house, when ye offer my bread, the fat and the blood, and they have broken my covenant because of all your abominations. And ye have not kept the charge of mine holy things: but ye have set keepers of my charge in my sanctuary for yourselves." Ezekiel 44:4-8.

The third section describes the duties of the Levites, who will be the caretakers of the millennial temple. The Levites were the tribe of Israelites descended from Jacob's son, Levi. The priests of Israel were a group of qualified men from within the tribe of the Levites who had responsibility for all the aspects of tabernacle or temple worship. All priests were to be Levites, according to the Law, but not all Levites were priests.

"Thus saith the Lord GOD; No stranger, uncircumcised in heart, nor uncircumcised in flesh, shall enter into my sanctuary, of any stranger that is among the children of Israel. And the Levites that are gone away far from me, when Israel went astray, which went astray away from me after their idols; they shall even bear their iniquity. Yet they shall be ministers in my

sanctuary, having charge at the gates of the house, and ministering to the house: they shall slay the burnt offering and the sacrifice for the people, and they shall stand before them to minister unto them. Because they ministered unto them before their idols, and caused the house of Israel to fall into iniquity; therefore have I lifted up mine hand against them, saith the Lord GOD, and they shall bear their iniquity. And they shall not come near unto me, to do the office of a priest unto me, nor to come near to any of my holy things, in the most holy place: but they shall bear their shame, and their abominations which they have committed. But I will make them keepers of the charge of the house, for all the service thereof, and for all that shall be done therein." Ezekiel 44:9-14.

"When the Jews received the Law of Moses at Sinai, the Lord gave commands regarding a formal priesthood for Israel. The priests would be males from the tribe of Levi and must meet certain physical and age qualifications in order to serve. In addition, they had to remain ceremonially clean to perform their duties before a holy God. The priests served as mediators between the Israelites and God. They were the ones who performed animal sacrifices on behalf of the people. It was only the priests who were permitted to enter the Holy Place in the tabernacle and, later, the temple." www.gotquestions.org.

In the fourth section, Ezekiel explains the duties of the sons of Zadok will be in charge of the sacrifices in the temple because of his loyalty to David when Absolom and Adonijah rebelled against their father.

Zadok, son of Ahitub, was a Levite priest during the time of King David. For a long time, he was a co-high priest with Abiathar. Zadok was a descendant of Aaron and a leader over his family of Levites.

*"But the priests the Levites, the sons of Zadok,
that kept the charge of my sanctuary when the
children of Israel went astray from me, they shall
come near to me to minister unto me, and they
shall stand before me to offer unto me the fat and
the blood, saith the Lord GOD: They shall enter
into my sanctuary, and they shall come near to my
table, to minister unto me, and they shall keep my
charge. And it shall come to pass, that when they
enter in at the gates of the inner court, they shall
be clothed with linen garments; and no wool shall
come upon them, whiles they minister in the gates
of the inner court, and within. They shall have
linen bonnets upon their heads, and shall have
linen breeches upon their loins; they shall not gird
themselves with any thing that causeth sweat. And
when they go forth into the utter court, even into
the utter court to the people, they shall put off
their garments wherein they ministered, and lay
them in the holy chambers, and they shall put on
other garments; and they shall not sanctify the
people with their garments. Neither shall they
shave their heads, nor suffer their locks to grow
long; they shall only poll their heads. Neither shall
any priest drink wine, when they enter into the
inner court. Neither shall they take for their wives
a widow, nor her that is put away: but they shall
take maidens of the seed of the house of Israel, or
a widow that had a priest before. And they shall
teach my people the difference between the holy
and profane, and cause them to discern between
the unclean and the clean. And in controversy
they shall stand in judgment; and they shall
judge it according to my judgments: and they*

shall keep my laws and my statutes in all mine assemblies; and they shall hallow my sabbaths. And they shall come at no dead person to defile themselves: but for father, or for mother, or for son, or for daughter, for brother, or for sister that hath had no husband, they may defile themselves. And after he is cleansed, they shall reckon unto him seven days. And in the day that he goeth into the sanctuary, unto the inner court, to minister in the sanctuary, he shall offer his sin offering, saith the Lord GOD. And it shall be unto them for an inheritance: I am their inheritance: and ye shall give them no possession in Israel: I am their possession. They shall eat the meat offering, and the sin offering, and the trespass offering; and every dedicated thing in Israel shall be theirs. And the first of all the firstfruits of all things, and every oblation of all, of every sort of your oblations, shall be the priest's: ye shall also give unto the priest the first of your dough, that he may cause the blessing to rest in thine house. The priests shall not eat of any thing that is dead of itself, or torn, whether it be fowl or beast." Ezekiel 44:15-31.

When Absalom conspired against his father, David, he forced David to flee from Jerusalem.

Zadok and his son Ahimaaz, and his co-priest Abiathar and his son Jonathan accompanied David, with Zadok leading a procession of Levites who carried the Ark of the Covenant. Once the people had vacated Jerusalem, David ordered Zadok and Abiathar, along with their sons, to return with the ark to Jerusalem. Zadok was to send word to David with any news of what was happening in the kingdom under Absalom.

Absalom planned to seek David and destroy him and the people who were with him. David escaped, and it wasn't much longer before David's commander, Joab, killed Absalom. Heartbroken at the death of his son, David returned to Jerusalem.

Years later, when King David was very old, his son Adonijah set himself up as king, even though David's other son Solomon was to take the throne at David's death. Adonijah had some supporters, including Abiathar, the priest, but Zadok, Nathan the prophet, and several other important men supported David's choice and opposed Adonijah. Nathan told David's wife Bathsheba what Adonijah was planning and advised her to apprise King David of the situation. She did so, and David ordered that Zadok and Nathan immediately take Solomon to Gihon and anoint him as king. When Zadok, the priest anointed Solomon's head with oil at Gihon, a trumpet was sounded, and all the people assembled began to shout and rejoice. The noise was so high that Adonijah, who was feasting nearby, heard it and wondered what was happening. At that moment, Abiathar's son Jonathan arrived and told Adonijah that Solomon had been anointed king. Adonijah fled to the temple and grabbed the horns of the altar, begging Solomon to spare his life. Solomon did so, but Adonijah later renewed his designs on the throne, forcing Solomon to execute him.

Even though Abiathar had spurned King David's wishes and supported Adonijah, Zadok stayed faithful to David and supported Solomon. Abiathar lost his priesthood as a result, but David rewarded Zadok with a position as one of Solomon's chief officials and being recognized as the sole high priest. Because of Zadok's faithfulness, his descendants will have charge over the Millennial Temple.

The fifth section describes the holy oblation for the mountain of Jehovah's house.

"Moreover, when ye shall divide by lot the land for inheritance, ye shall offer an oblation unto the LORD, an holy portion of the land: the length shall be the length of five and twenty thousand

reeds, and the breadth shall be ten thousand. This shall be holy in all the borders thereof round about. Of this there shall be for the sanctuary five hundred in length, with five hundred in breadth, square round about; and fifty cubits round about for the suburbs thereof. And of this measure shalt thou measure the length of five and twenty thousand, and the breadth of ten thousand: and in it shall be the sanctuary and the most holy place. The holy portion of the land shall be for the priests the ministers of the sanctuary, which shall come near to minister unto the LORD: and it shall be a place for their houses and an holy place for the sanctuary. And the five and twenty thousand of length, and the ten thousand of breadth, shall also the Levites, the ministers of the house, have for themselves, for a possession for twenty chambers. And ye shall appoint the possession of the city five thousand broad, and five and twenty thousand long, over against the oblation of the holy portion: it shall be for the whole house of Israel. And a portion shall be for the prince on the one side and on the other side of the oblation of the holy portion, and of the possession of the city, before the oblation of the holy portion, and before the possession of the city, from the west side westward, and from the east side eastward: and the length shall be over against one of the portions, from the west border unto the east border. In the land shall be his possession in Israel: and my princes shall no more oppress my people; and the rest of the land shall they give to the house of Israel according to their tribes." Ezekiel 45:1-8.

Next, Ezekiel describes the duties of the Prince, David.

"Thus saith the Lord GOD; Let it suffice you, O princes of Israel: remove violence and spoil, and execute judgment and justice, take away your exactions from my people, saith the Lord GOD. Ye shall have just balances, and a just ephah, and a just bath. The ephah and the bath shall be of one measure, that the bath may contain the tenth part of an homer, and the ephah the tenth part of an homer: the measure thereof shall be after the homer. And the shekel shall be twenty gerahs: twenty shekels, five and twenty shekels, fifteen shekels, shall be your maneh. This is the oblation that ye shall offer; the sixth part of an ephah of an homer of wheat, and ye shall give the sixth part of an ephah of an homer of barley: Concerning the ordinance of oil, the bath of oil, ye shall offer the tenth part of a bath out of the cor, which is an homer of ten baths; for ten baths are an homer: And one lamb out of the flock, out of two hundred, out of the fat pastures of Israel; for a meat offering, and for a burnt offering, and for peace offerings, to make reconciliation for them, saith the Lord GOD. All the people of the land shall give this oblation for the prince in Israel. And it shall be the prince's part to give burnt offerings, and meat offerings, and drink offerings, in the feasts, and in the new moons, and in the sabbaths, in all solemnities of the house of Israel: he shall prepare the sin offering, and the meat offering, and the burnt offering, and the peace offerings, to make reconciliation for the house of Israel. Thus saith the Lord GOD;

In the first month, in the first day of the month, thou shalt take a young bullock without blemish, and cleanse the sanctuary:" Ezekiel 45:9-18.

Truth and honesty will characterize the law of measurement. The responsibilities will involve the carrying out of the law of offerings, including the new year offerings, the Passover offerings, the offerings for the feast of Tabernacles, and the Sabbath offerings. The Prince will have some exclusive rights because of his exalted position concerning the Temple.

The last section (Ezekiel 46:19-24) concerns the Ark of the Covenant.

"One of the things in Solomon's temple that will be absent in the Millennial Temple is the Ark of the covenant." Arnold Fruchtenbaum.

"And the priest shall take of the blood of the sin offering, and put it upon the posts of the house, and upon the four corners of the settle of the altar, and upon the posts of the gate of the inner court. And so thou shalt do the seventh day of the month for every one that erreth, and for him that is simple: so shall ye reconcile the house. In the first month, in the fourteenth day of the month, ye shall have the Passover, a feast of seven days; unleavened bread shall be eaten. And upon that day shall the prince prepare for himself and for all the people of the land a bullock for a sin offering. And seven days of the feast he shall prepare a burnt offering to the LORD, seven bullocks and seven rams without blemish daily the seven days; and a kid of the goats daily for a sin offering. And he shall prepare a meat offering of an ephah for a bullock, and an ephah for a ram, and an hin of oil for an ephah." Ezekiel 45:19-24.

> *"And it shall come to pass, when ye be multiplied and increased in the land, in those days, saith the LORD, they shall say no more, The ark of the covenant of the LORD: neither shall it come to mind: neither shall they remember it; neither shall they visit it; neither shall that be done any more." Jeremiah3:16.*

"Since God himself in the person of the Messiah will be dwelling in and reigning from Jerusalem, there will be no need for any Ark of the Covenant. Furthermore, the Ark of the Covenant contained the tablets of stone that were the embodiment of the Law of Moses. The fact that the Law of Moses is no longer in effect is another reason that the Ark of the Covenant will be missing." Dr. Arnold Fruchtenbaum

There will be a brand-new sacrificial system in the millennium. It will contain some features similar to the Mosaic system but also have new things instituted for an entirely different purpose. One reason for Millennial sacrifices is to memorialize the death of the Messiah. These sacrifices will play for Israel a similar role in that communion plays for the Church. The Mosaic sacrifices looked forward to the sacrifice of the Messiah; the Kingdom sacrifices look back and commemorate His sacrifice on the cross at Calvary.

The millennial sacrifices will not take away sin, but they will be the means of restoring fellowship for the millennial Saint who sins.

The sacrifices will provide a means of ritual cleansing. Since the Shekinah Glory will be within the Holy of Holies of The Millennial Temple, it would be impossible to approach the Temple compound in the state of ritual impurity. Therefore the sacrifices will be for the cleansing of ceremonial uncleanness.

Ezekiel describes the worship that occurs at the temple during Messiah's Millennial Reign.

> *"Thus saith the Lord GOD; The gate of the inner court that looketh toward the east shall be shut*

the six working days; but on the sabbath it shall be opened, and in the day of the new moon it shall be opened. And the prince shall enter by the way of the porch of that gate without, and shall stand by the post of the gate, and the priests shall prepare his burnt offering and his peace offerings, and he shall worship at the threshold of the gate: then he shall go forth; but the gate shall not be shut until the evening. Likewise the people of the land shall worship at the door of this gate before the LORD in the sabbaths and in the new moons. And the burnt offering that the prince shall offer unto the LORD in the sabbath day shall be six lambs without blemish, and a ram without blemish. And the meat offering shall be an ephah for a ram, and the meat offering for the lambs as he shall be able to give, and an hin of oil to an ephah. And in the day of the new moon it shall be a young bullock without blemish, and six lambs, and a ram: they shall be without blemish." Ezekiel 46:1-6.

"The point is that God's methodology is not and will not change. These "appointed times" where fixed at the beginning and for all time. Therefore they will be observed and celebrated during the Millennium just as they were celebrated centuries ago. Therefore I suggest that if they were relevant in the past and will be relevant in the future, they are also relevant presently! Should we not pay attention to God's appointed times and seasons and learn the lessons they teach us and especially since they teach us of the Messiah and all that God intends for his people?" Perry Stone Jr.

7

𝔑ew 𝔚orld 𝔈conomy

*And they shall build houses, and inhabit them;
and they shall plant vineyards and eat the fruit of
them. They shall not build, and another inhabit;
they shall not plant, and another eat: for as the
days of a tree are the days of my people, and mine
elect shall long enjoy the work of their hands.
They shall not labour in vain, nor bring forth
for trouble; for they are the seed of the blessed of
the LORD, and their offspring with them. And
it shall come to pass, that before they call, I will
answer; and while they are yet speaking, I will
hear." Isiah 65:21-24.*

We have been looking at the structure, government, population, and religious practice of the Millennial. But what will life be like while living in the thousand-year reign of Jesus the Messiah? Satan, in this world, would have us believe that we will spend eternity beginning with the return of Christ floating on clouds and strumming harps. I've never played the harp, and I doubt that the clouds would hold my weight besides something like that seems to be boring. And that would be against everything the Lord said about his kingdom.

> *"But as it is written, Eye hath not seen, nor ear heard, neither have entered into the heart of man, the things which God hath prepared for them that love him." 1 Corinthians 2:9*

Life in the kingdom will be anything but boring. God has resurrected his original creation, and humanity is once again put in the position of managing God's world. Remember, in Genesis chapter one, *"the Lord took the man and put him into the garden of Eden dress it and to keep it."* Adam and Eve had work to do to keep the garden beautiful and flourishing.

God's Reconstruction Program:

When the millennium begins, the world will be in shambles, having suffered through the judgments of Satan's rule. When Jesus appears, the restoration of this planet will start so that He may reign for a thousand years.

"As said, Jerusalem, Mount Zion, Israel, and the planet, by means of physical convulsion and geological changes suddenly effected through disruption, depression, fissure, and elevation, at the Moshiach's appearing, shall be utterly changed. Jerusalem and Mount Zion shall be exalted or lifted high, above the surrounding hills, and the adjacent region be reduced to a plain, like the Arabah, or Ghor, that runs from the slopes of Hermon to the Red Sea. All the land will change itself, and the geographic centre of the reconstruction will be determined by the boundaries of the ancient territory of Judah.

All this is the effect of the Presence (Shekinah) of HaShem (the

Name), more awful than His Presence at Sinai. After all the changes, rains shall come in the correct seasons, and the land shall be fruitful. Bounteous harvests will result as the land becomes fruitful. Broad rivers and streams will cover the lands, turning the deserts into gardens. Beautiful trees shall replace briars and thorns. The land shall be so beautiful that the earth before will not even come to mind. The waste places and destroyed cities shall be rebuilt and inhabited.

Specifically, the Dead Sea shall be healed and shall team with fish. Living waters shall spring forth upon the earth, and it shall become like the Garden of Eden. The beautification of Lebanon seems to have made a great impression. Lebanon must play a pivotal role in the invasion of Israel to warrant such complete desolation and subsequent rebirth. The areas of Sharon and Achor (within Israel) shall be pastures for flocks and herds. These areas are mostly barren desert now. The longstanding curse will be lifted." Prof. (Dr.) WA. Liebenberg.

The world needs to be rebuilt, and Jesus will assign people with the skills to reestablish his New World order. He will use people to design and build all the necessary equipment and products to rebuild churches, homes, factories, and recreational facilities. He will need not only physical laborers but also managers, innovators, designers, planners, architects, and project managers to do the reconstruction of this world.

God promises that the land will bring forth abundantly, so he will need farmers to cultivate, plant, and harvest the food that the world will need.

During the Millennium, farmers will grow crops; ranchers will raise cattle without having to fight the earth or insects or predators and disease.

> **"And I will raise up for them a plant of renown, and they shall be no more consumed with hunger in the land, neither bear the shame of the heathen any more." Ezekiel 34:29.**

"There something deeply stirring about seeing magnificent fields of ripe grain and orchards of fruit-laden trees. Have you ever seen the acres of blossoming tulips in Holland? The explosion of luxuriant trees and foliage in the South Pacific islands is also breathtaking! Wild coconuts, bananas, and papaya seem like a foretaste of the millennium. Sometimes I think God put these unspoiled islands out there to give us a hint of verdant eternity," George Otis Sr.

Also, the world will need skilled individuals to handle the logistics of farm to table transportation of food supplies, and raw materials, to factories, to warehouses to retail outlets and eventually to the citizens of God's New World order.

Righteous Leaders:

Also, His government will require leaders of neighborhoods and towns and states and even countries. All these are working in accordance with the will of Christ to build the beautiful world that He has promised.

But there's more to meet man's needs than just food and shelter. We also require music, entertainment, athletic competition, and educational pursuits to keep our mind and emotions in a proper balance.

That's a lot that has to be done to re-establish a new society. But when you consider the length of a lifetime in the millennium will be much longer than the threescore and ten, we live with today. In the millennium, they will consider a person who dies 100 years old a mere youngster because of the perfect environment that will exist. The longevity of human life will be like those recorded in the first few chapters of Genesis. Just imagine what you could accomplish in a lifespan of 700 to 900 years without the influence of sin and sickness.

"The meek and poor of spirit will be lifted and shall rejoice in HaShem. The blind and deaf shall be healed, the lame man shall leap like a deer, and the tongues of the dumb shall sing. All diseases and disabilities shall be done away with. The righteous shall have renewed

strength and endurance and shall follow HaShem with great rejoice.
They will live in peace and safety under the protective arm of HaShem."
Prof. (Dr.) WA. Liebenberg.

Advanced Technology:

Neurosurgeons suggest that the human brain is now functioning at less than 7% of its design capacity. Just imagine what we could accomplish when our full mental capabilities are turned loose in science and technology.

Arthur Longley has comprehended this new mental energy believers will soon experience.

"Suddenly, at the rapture, Christians will inherit a life force that will stimulate the brain to high levels of intelligence, capable of grappling with the problems that now baffle the world's greatest minds." Arthur Longley.

God's New World Order also will see technical breakthroughs providing the New World with inexhaustible, pollution-free energy. Scientists know that a glass of water has more potential energy locked in it's molecular structures than a million barrels of oil or 100,000 tons of coal. We just don't know how to unlock it.

"Congestion, accidents, and pollution are consequences of our overcrowded streets and groaning transportation systems. 20th-century man still travels almost exclusively in one hilly, congested plane - the Earth's surface. This will be corrected. Even with the thousands of aircraft now flying, our skies are still largely unused. There are hundreds of additional transportation corridors of the air above us.

We will be traveling these airways in public supersonic airbuses or our own nifty air cars. This will enable us to swiftly and effortlessly go anywhere. We will see new engines, advanced metallurgy, even tinier computers, more advanced navigation satellites, laser landing systems, and revolutionized aerodynamics. Fast and easy to fly vehicles will be as easy to build as our mass-produced automobiles.

It isn't difficult to realize a six-passenger supersonic air car that would be driven as easily as we do now pilot our own cars. With automated flight controls and landing systems, it will be possible to program Beijing for lunch and be on our way. Millennial air cars will hover and land effortlessly, parking in our own garage."

Computers will direct beautiful freighters, perhaps a mile long through their own assigned air corridors. They will move fresh food, materials, and even houses --- playing their part ideal logistics and distribution of all the millennial civilization." George Otis Sr.

> **"But as it is written, Eye hath not seen, nor ear heard, neither have entered into the heart of man, the things which God hath prepared for them that love him." 1 Corinthians 2:9.**

Peace on Earth, finally:

Wholesome will replace the present fascination with violent news. It won't be popular to broadcast sex, war, famine, rape, robbery, riots, rebellions, including the actions of corrupt politicians and dishonest Fake News. Once again, their stories will be of good events and encouragements.

We will know the Bible personalities:

> **"... And it came to pass about an eight days after these sayings, he took Peter and John and James, and went up into a mountain to pray. And as he prayed, the fashion of his countenance was altered, and his raiment was white and glistering. And, behold, there talked with him two men, which were Moses and Elias: Who appeared in glory, and spake of his decease which he should accomplish at**

Jerusalem. But Peter and they that were with him were heavy with sleep: and when they were awake, they saw his glory and the two men that stood with him. And it came to pass, as they departed from him, Peter said unto Jesus, Master, it is good for us to be here: and let us make three tabernacles; one for thee, and one for Moses, and one for Elias: not knowing what he said. While he thus spake, there came a cloud, and overshadowed them: and they feared as they entered into the cloud. And there came a voice out of the cloud, saying, This is my beloved Son: hear him. And when the voice was past, Jesus was found alone. And they kept it close, and told no man in those days any of those things which they had seen." Luke 9:28-36.

When the disciples met Elijah and Moses on Mount of Transfiguration, they instantly recognized them. They needed no introductions. In the Millennium, the Bible says that we will *"... know as even as I also am known."* We will have memories that will allow us to remember dates, anniversaries, appointments, the names of everyone dwelling in God's New World.

"For then will I turn to the people a pure language, that they may all call upon the name of the LORD, to serve him with one consent." Zephaniah 3:9.

Another exciting change for humanity during the Millennium will be a new language, as the 6,700 languages in the world today will be reduced to a single language for all humanity. The confusion that God sent at the tower of Babel will be removed, and everyone will speak God's language.

8

New World Environment

"The wolf and the lamb shall feed together, and the lion shall eat straw like the bullock: and dust shall be the serpent's meat. They shall not hurt nor destroy in all my holy mountain, saith the LORD." Isiah 65:25.

This passage from Isaiah describes the new heaven and the new earth of the renovated Earth. The result will be a continuation of many things of the old universe and some new ones. Israel will undergo a significant renovation process. Some elements of the old order will remain, such as the Mediterranean Sea and the Dead Sea. But several things will be brand-new, such as the exceedingly high mountain in the center of the country.

"There shall be no more thence an infant of days, nor an old man that hath not filled his days: for the child shall die an hundred years old; but

> *the sinner being an hundred years old shall be*
> *accursed." Isaiah 65:20.*

"Verse 20 is especially significant, for it discusses life and death in the kingdom. This verse teaches many things. First: there will no longer be any infant mortality in the millennium; everyone who is born in the kingdom will reach a certain age. Second: the specific age at which one may die is the age of 100. With infant mortality removed, everyone born in the millennium will live at least until their 100ᵗʰ year of life. Because of the prolongation of life in the millennium, those who die at the age of 100 will be considered as having died young. Third: this verse limits the people dying at the age of 100 to those who are sinners; namely, unbelievers, as only they would be considered a cursed. So, then, death in the kingdom will be for unbelievers only." Dr. Arnold Fruchtenbaum.

Newly born, people will inherit the sin nature from their natural parents and will require regeneration. Although Satan will be bound during this period, the inherent sin nature can rebel against God. Thus there will be unsaved people living in the kingdom in need of regeneration. That means salvation by grace through faith in the substitutionary death of the Messiah/Jesus for sin and his subsequent resurrection. It appears that those born in the kingdom will have until their 100ᵗʰ year to believe. God may not allow an unbeliever to live past his first century of life. However, if they repent and believe in Jesus' substitutionary sacrifice for their sins, they will live throughout the millennium and never die.

A time of personal peace and prosperity:

It will be a time of building and planting, with guaranteed results for the builder and the farmer. They all enjoy the results of their labor. Much of the Edenic curse will be removed.

Longevity, absence of calamity and turmoil, and instantaneous response from God will characterize life. The animal kingdom will be at peace with each other and with man.

"The Tribal people of Israel shall be a righteous and industrious people. They shall make merry and will multiply, blossom and bud. None shall make them afraid." Prof. (Dr.) WA. Liebenberg.

Millennial Employment & Working:

In the Messiah's resurrected world, we will still need to work, but gone from the work will be the tediousness drudgery and the strife between coworkers. We will exercise our full mental capacities for the improvement of the planet and our existence.

There will be manufacturing plants that will take the implements of war from the campaign of Armageddon and turn them into machinery, tractors, bulldozers, cranes, and other construction machines.

We won't have to worry about the pollution of the sea and air, and the water will be as pure as when God created it in Genesis. Streams, wells and fountains will all be freshwaters. Hurricanes, tornadoes, cyclones, and other disasters will simply not exist in God's restored world. It will be just like God described in Genesis. *"Very good."*

> *"And God said, Behold, I have given you every herb bearing seed, which is upon the face of all the earth, and every tree, in the which is the fruit of a tree yielding seed; to you, it shall be for meat. And to every beast of the earth, and to every fowl of the air, and to every thing that creepeth upon the earth, wherein there is life, I have given every green herb for meat: and it was so. And God saw every thing that he had made, and, behold, it was*

very good. And the evening and the morning were the sixth day." Genesis 1:29-31.

My wife and I like to watch the various animal shows on television. God created a lot of beautiful creatures, and some just plain interesting. There's nothing more attractive than a baby animal, no matter what specie. I'd love to have them all as pets, but the curse placed on the world would not safely allow that. But someday soon that too will change.

> *"The wolf also shall dwell with the lamb, and the leopard shall lie down with the kid; and the calf and the young lion and the fatling together; and a little child shall lead them. And the cow and the bear shall feed; their young ones shall lie down together: and the lion shall eat straw like the ox. And the sucking child shall play on the hole of the asp, and the weaned child shall put his hand on the cockatrice' den. They shall not hurt nor destroy in all my holy mountain: for the earth shall be full of the knowledge of the LORD, as the waters cover the sea." Isaiah 11:6-9.*

And wars will be no more. In millennium nations will not need armies to protect their borders or their peoples. They will not need fences and locks and walls to protect their wealth and resources. The world will be a world of righteousness controlled by the righteousness of the Holy Messiah, Jesus. He will settle any strife or division through a holy judicial process without the need for any violence. No more riots. No more rebellions. No more political mudslinging. Just world peace.

> *"And he shall judge among many people, and rebuke strong nations afar off; and they shall*

beat their swords into plowshares, and their spears into pruninghooks: nation shall not lift up a sword against nation, neither shall they learn war any more." Micah 4:3.

Education in the new millennium will be an enjoyable process. Each child learns at a different pace so that learning will be on an individualized basis. Because our brains will work at 100%, education will be much more comfortable and less tedious than it is today. Complicated subjects which we avoid now we will want to explore. Learning will also be in accordance with our innate abilities and talents, as God has given to each one of us. We will use our skills to their fullest capacity. And since lifetimes are more prolonged than now, just imagine how much you can accomplish if your lifespan was ten times or more years versus the present threescore and ten.

Science will be taught with the secrets of God and will not have the influence of man-made theories such as evolution and gender perversion.

9

New World Government

"Yet have I set my king upon my holy hill of Zion. I will declare the decree: the LORD hath said unto me, Thou art my Son; this day have I begotten thee. Ask of me, and I shall give thee the heathen for thine inheritance, and the uttermost parts of the earth for thy possession." Psalm 2:6-8.

When Jesus Christ returns to earth, He will establish the Kingdom of God in Jerusalem over "all peoples, nations, and languages."

"I saw in the night visions, and, behold, one like the Son of man came with the clouds of heaven, and came to the Ancient of days, and they brought him near before him. And there was given him dominion, and glory, and a kingdom, that all people, nations, and languages, should serve him: his dominion is an everlasting dominion,

which shall not pass away, and his kingdom that
which shall not be destroyed." Daniel 7:13-14.

The entire earth will be under the dominion of His government! He will take control of all the governments of this earth.

"And the seventh angel sounded; and there were
great voices in heaven, saying, the kingdoms of
this world are become the kingdoms of our Lord,
and of his Christ; and he shall reign for ever and
ever." Revelation 11:15.

That is why the message of the Kingdom is called the gospel—or *the good news*! Under the rule of Jesus Christ, a perfect leader who administers in truth and justice will rule the world. His law will be taught to all and will bring peace and happiness to human beings on earth.

"The word that Isaiah, the son of Amoz, saw
concerning Judah and Jerusalem. And it shall
come to pass in the last days, that the mountain
of the LORD'S house shall be established in the
top of the mountains, and shall be exalted above
the hills; and all nations shall flow unto it. And
many people shall go and say, Come ye, and let us
go up to the mountain of the LORD, to the house
of the God of Jacob; and he will teach us of his
ways, and we will walk in his paths: for out of
Zion shall go forth the law, and the word of the
LORD from Jerusalem." Isaiah 2:1-3.

The righteousness of its citizens will characterize the kingdom of God in the millennium. Although not every citizen will be categorized as righteous, most will be. Isaiah describes one of the significant characteristics of the messianic kingdom, that of universal peace.

> *"And it shall come to pass in the last days, that the mountain of the LORD'S house shall be established in the top of the mountains, and shall be exalted above the hills; and all nations shall flow unto it. And many people shall go and say, Come ye, and let us go up to the mountain of the LORD, to the house of the God of Jacob; and he will teach us of his ways, and we will walk in his paths: for out of Zion shall go forth the law, and the word of the LORD from Jerusalem. And he shall judge among the nations, and shall rebuke many people: and they shall beat their swords into plowshares, and their spears into pruninghooks: nation shall not lift up sword against nation, neither shall they learn war any more." Isaiah 2:2-4.*

Disputes will still arise between nations, but they will no longer be settled by armed conflict but will be settled by the word of the Lord from Jerusalem. They will forget the art of war during Jesus' reign.

"The universal peace described earlier will extend even to the animal kingdom. All animals will return to the Edenic state and become vegetarians. The oldest of enemies, man, and snakes, will be able to live in compatibility in that day, for the knowledge of God will permeate throughout the entire world, affecting man and animal alike." Randy Alcorn.

Jerusalem will draw all nations unto it.

Jerusalem will also be a focus of attention of all the Gentile nations.

> *"Thus saith the LORD of hosts; It shall yet come*
> *to pass, that there shall come people, and the*
> *inhabitants of many cities: And the inhabitants*
> *of one city shall go to another, saying, Let us go*
> *speedily to pray before the LORD, and to seek the*
> *LORD of hosts: I will go also. Yea, many people,*
> *and strong nations shall come to seek the LORD*
> *of hosts in Jerusalem and to pray before the*
> *LORD. Thus saith the LORD of hosts; In those*
> *days it shall come to pass, that ten men shall take*
> *hold out of all languages of the nations, even*
> *shall take hold of the skirt of him that is a Jew,*
> *saying, We will go with you: for we have heard*
> *that God is with you." Zechariah 8:20-22.*

Messiah/Jesus will be the king of the city, and the very land around it will be significantly altered so that Jerusalem can be enlarged and exalted on the mountain of Jehovah's house. And once Messiah dwells there, the city will be truly called the *"city of peace"* and will finally live-in total security.

After defeating the armies of the Antichrist and incarcerating Satan to his thousand-year confinement for rebellion against God, Jesus, the Messiah, will reign as the theocratic ruler of the world. He will have an organized government comprising two branches. One branch will administer the Gentile nations with the Church and the Tribulation Saints as the leaders. They will rule over the kings of every country and all the Gentiles. The Twelve Apostles will head the Jewish branch of government and have charge over the princes, judges, and counselors of Israel.

> *"Yet have I set my king upon my holy hill of Zion. I*
> *will declare the decree: the LORD hath said unto*
> *me, Thou art my Son; this day have I begotten*
> *thee. Ask of me, and I shall give thee the heathen*

> *for thine inheritance, and the uttermost parts of*
> *the earth for thy possession." Psalms 2:6-8.*

"Although the throne of David the Messiah will be established in Jerusalem, his domain will not stop at the border of Israel, but will extend throughout the entire earth with every Gentile nation falling under his domain." Arnold Fruchtenbaum.

His Messianic Kingdom will fulfill the prophecy of Psalms 2:6-8 of him sitting on the throne of David. Christians often quote this at Christmas.

> *"Then shall he speak unto them in his wrath, and*
> *vex them in his sore displeasure. Yet have I set*
> *my king upon my holy hill of Zion. I will declare*
> *the decree: the LORD hath said unto me, Thou*
> *art my Son; this day have I begotten thee. Ask of*
> *me, and I shall give thee the heathen for thine*
> *inheritance, and the uttermost parts of the earth*
> *for thy possession." Psalm 2:5-8.*

Luke tells us of this message sent to the Virgin Mary by the angel Gabriel.

> *"And the angel said unto her, Fear not, Mary: for*
> *thou hast found favour with God. And, behold,*
> *thou shalt conceive in thy womb and bring forth*
> *a son, and shalt call his name JESUS. He shall be*
> *great, and shall be called the Son of the Highest:*
> *and the Lord God shall give unto him the throne*
> *of his father David: And he shall reign over the*
> *house of Jacob for ever; and of his kingdom, there*
> *shall be no end." Luke 1:30-33.*

This announcement by Gabriel concerning Jesus as the king on

David's throne is rooted in prophecies of the Davidic Covenant and other prophecies in the Old Testament.

Revelation twice informs us that his reign as Messiah-King will stem from an absolute monarchy and that he will rule with a rod of iron. (Revelation 12:5 and 19:15). This iron hand is rooted in Psalm 2:9.

> *"Thou shalt break them with a rod of iron; thou shalt dash them in pieces like a potter's vessel."* *Psalm 2:9.*

Jesus' return to Jerusalem:

When Jesus rode into Jerusalem on Palm Sunday riding on a donkey, He was hailed with *"Hosanna to the son of David: Blessed is he that cometh in the name of the Lord; Hosanna in the highest."* by the multitude. Four days later, the same multitude was shouting to *"crucify him."* This time when Jesus the Messiah enters Jerusalem, he will ride on a white horse as a conqueror, and every knee shall bow allegiance to him to the glory of God the Father.

> *"And I saw heaven opened, and behold a white horse; and he that sat upon him was called Faithful and True, and in righteousness he doth judge and make war. His eyes were as a flame of fire, and on his head were many crowns; and he had a name written, that no man knew, but he himself. And he was clothed with a vesture dipped in blood: and his name is called The Word of God. And the armies which were in heaven followed him upon white horses, clothed in fine linen, white and clean. And out of his mouth goeth a sharp sword, that with it he should*

> *smite the nations: and he shall rule them with*
> *a rod of iron: and he treadeth the winepress of*
> *the fierceness and wrath of Almighty God. And*
> *he hath on his vesture and on his thigh a name*
> *written, KING OF KINGS, AND LORD OF*
> *LORDS." Revelation 19:11-16.*

The Resurrected Church and the Tribulation Saints will reign with Messiah/Jesus over the Gentile nations. They will be Messiah's representative authority to carry out his decrees to all the countries of the world. Individual kings will be the rulers of their own nations. However, they will be under the authority of the Church and the Tribulation Saints.

The Theocracy of Jesus the Messiah:

"A theocracy is a form of government in which a deity of some type is recognized as the supreme ruling authority, giving divine guidance to human intermediaries that manage the day-to-day affairs of the government." Wikipedia.

The absolute theocracy of the Messiah will be over Israel and the Gentile nations. Under the authority of the Messiah will be the resurrected King David to rule over Israel.

> *"And I will set up one shepherd over them, and he*
> *shall feed them, even my servant David; he shall*
> *feed them, and he shall be their shepherd. And*
> *I the LORD will be their God, and my servant*
> *David a prince among them; I the LORD have*
> *spoken it." Ezekiel 34:23-24.*

Jesus promised his twelve apostles that in the kingdom, they would be in authority over the twelve tribes.

*"And Jesus said unto them, Verily I say unto
you, That ye which have followed me, in the
regeneration when the Son of man shall sit in the
throne of his glory, ye also shall sit upon twelve
thrones, judging the twelve tribes of Israel."
Matthew 19:28.*

And also:

*"Ye are they which have continued with me in my
temptations. And I appoint unto you a kingdom,
as my Father hath appointed unto me; That ye
may eat and drink at my table in my kingdom,
and sit on thrones judging the twelve tribes of
Israel." Luke 22:28-30.*

The authority over the kingdom, the Father, gave to the Son,
Jesus passed on to his twelve apostles. Messiah Jesus's domain will
be over the world, David's rule over all of Israel, while the apostles
will have jurisdiction over the Tribes of Israel.

Besides these, the Bible also mentions princes and judges and
counselors who will be part of Jesus's government. Israel is also to
become the head over the Gentiles.

According to Scripture, Jesus, the Messiah, will sit upon the
throne of David and rule the kingdom of Israel with his dominion
extending all over the Gentile world. The Bible speaks of the Davidic
covenant and Messiah as king over a literal global kingdom on earth.
The Bible teaches God's son will be king in Jerusalem.

*"Yet have I set my king upon my holy hill of Zion. I
will declare the decree: the LORD hath said unto
me, Thou art my Son; this day have I begotten
thee. Ask of me, and I shall give thee the heathen
for thine inheritance, and the uttermost parts of
the earth for thy possession." Psalm 2:6-8.*

Isaiah declares again that a throne will be established based on God's loyal love for David. The one sitting on the throne will be a member of the house of David, who will be characterized by truth. He will be king and judge, ensuring that justice is carried out. This justice comes from the righteousness of King Jesus. The one ruling over David's throne is the God-man, Yeshua. Wisdom, justice, and righteousness will characterize his reign.

"And the LORD shall be king over all the earth: in that day shall there be one LORD, and his name one." Zechariah 14:9

Luke, in the New Testament, declares the establishment of the Davidic throne with Messiah reigning from Jerusalem.

"And the angel said unto her, Fear not, Mary: for thou hast found favour with God. And, behold, thou shalt conceive in thy womb, and bring forth a son, and shalt call his name JESUS. He shall be great, and shall be called the Son of the Highest: and the Lord God shall give unto him the throne of his father David: And he shall reign over the house of Jacob for ever; and of his kingdom there shall be no end." Luke 1:30-33.

Gabriel declares to Mary that her son born into the Jewish world and is to sit on David's throne as the God-man. He is the Son of God and also a descendent of King David. The Son will be given the throne of David by divine appointment. He is to reign over Israel, and there will be no end to his rule. His reign is rooted in the Old Testament prophecies of the Davidic covenant.

"And out of his mouth goeth a sharp sword, that with it he should smite the nations: and he shall

> *rule them with a rod of iron: and he treadeth the winepress of the fierceness and wrath of Almighty God. And he hath on his vesture and on his thigh a name written, KING OF KINGS, AND LORD OF LORDS." Revelation 19:15-16.*

This iron-handed rule is rooted in Psalm 2:9 and will be necessary because nations will exist, and the people populating them will still have their sinful nature. The natural outworking of this sinful nature will have to be restrained. The kingdom will not be a democracy but an absolute monarchy. The reign of the messianic king will be a strict one, and the righteous and just laws emulating from Jerusalem will have to be obeyed because Jesus will rule with a rod of iron in justice, righteousness, holiness, where faithfulness will be rewarded. Any sinful activity will be severely rectified. As both king of Israel and King of the World, his absolute authority and monarchy will have two branches of government established. The Gentile branch and the Jewish branch.

The Gentile Branch:

> *"And I saw thrones, and they sat upon them, and judgment was given unto them: and I saw the souls of them that were beheaded for the witness of Jesus, and for the word of God, and which had not worshipped the beast, neither his image, neither had received his mark upon their foreheads, or in their hands; and they lived and reigned with Christ a thousand years. But the rest of the dead lived not again until the thousand years were finished. This is the first resurrection. Blessed and holy is he that hath part in the first resurrection: on such the second*

death hath no power, but they shall be priests of God and of Christ, and shall reign with him a thousand years." Revelation 20:4-6.

John describes the saints who will reign with Jesus. These raptured saints have already been judged before the great tribulation. This judgment was at the bema seat of the Messiah, which judged the believer's works. The outcome of this judgment will determine the positions of each church saint in the kingdom. The second group of saints who will reign with Him are those that martyred during the first half of the tribulation and were sealed under the fifth seal.

"And when he had opened the fifth seal, I saw under the altar the souls of them that were slain for the word of God, and for the testimony which they held:" Revelation 6:9.

The third group is those who did not receive the mark 666 of the beast in the forehead or right hand. Both the church saints and the tribulation saints will co-rule with the king for 1000 years in their glorified bodies.

"The Gentile nations will have Kings over them. These kings will have their natural bodies while the saints who will be over them will have their spiritual, resurrected and glorified bodies while the individual kings will be the supreme rulers of their own nations, they themselves will be under the authority of the church and tribulation saints." Dr. Arnold Fruchtenbaum.

The Jewish branch:

Directly under the Messiah, and having authority over all of Israel, will be the resurrected King David. He will govern Israel's 12 tribes under the direction of Messiah Jesus. While the Gentile kings will all have natural bodies, David will have a glorified resurrected body.

> *"Therefore will I save my flock, and they shall no more be a prey; and I will judge between cattle and cattle. And I will set up one shepherd over them, and he shall feed them, even my servant David; he shall feed them, and he shall be their shepherd. And I the LORD will be their God, and my servant David a prince among them; I the LORD have spoken it." Ezekiel 34:22-24.*

"So while Jehovah will serve as their God and absolute king, David will serve under him as God's prince over Israel." Dr. Arnold Fruchtenbaum

Ezekiel reveals the fact that they will have David as their king. He is also to be their prince and shepherd. Hosea says that in the future restoration, Israel will not only be of subservient to Jehovah their God but also David, their king.

The Twelve Apostles Rule the Twelve Tribes:

Jesus, on two occasions, promised his twelve apostles that in the kingdom, they would rule over the twelve tribes of Israel.

> *"And Jesus said unto them, Verily I say unto you, That ye which have followed me, in the regeneration when the Son of man shall sit in the throne of his glory, ye also shall sit upon twelve thrones, judging the twelve tribes of Israel." Matthew 19:28.*

The regeneration used here refers to the renovation of the earth. Jesus will sit upon the re-established throne of David in his glory. It is then that Yeshua sets the 12 thrones up, one over each of the 12 tribes where the apostles will exercise their authority. Thus messiahs domain will be over the entire world; David's rule through the apostles will be over Israel. It will be interesting to find out which apostle has the jurisdiction over which tribe as the Bible does not disclose that information.

Princes:

Isaiah 32:1 and Ezekiel 45:8 references other rulers who are similarly titled as princes. These princes will have positions of authority in the millennium. Involved in their jurisdiction will be the partitioning of the land of Israel into its 12 tribal divisions.

> *"Behold, a king shall reign in righteousness, and princes shall rule in judgment." Isaiah 32:1*

> *"In the land shall be his possession in Israel: and my princes shall no more oppress my people; and the rest of the land shall they give to the house of Israel according to their tribes." Ezekiel 45:8.*

Judges:

The authority of judges and counselors will be related to the city of Jerusalem. They will be responsible for dispensing of justice and judicial decisions, and through them, there will be no perversion of justice.

> *"And I will restore thy judges as at the first, and thy counsellers as at the beginning: afterward thou shalt be called, The city of righteousness, the faithful city." Isaiah 1:26.*

10

New World Rebellion

"And when the thousand years are expired, Satan shall be loosed out of his prison," Revelation 20:7.

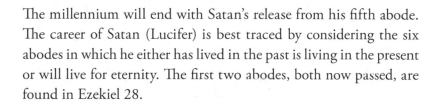

The millennium will end with Satan's release from his fifth abode. The career of Satan (Lucifer) is best traced by considering the six abodes in which he either has lived in the past is living in the present or will live for eternity. The first two abodes, both now passed, are found in Ezekiel 28.

> *"Moreover, the word of the LORD came unto me, saying, Son of man, take up a lamentation upon the king of Tyrus, and say unto him, Thus saith the Lord GOD; Thou sealest up the sum, full of wisdom, and perfect in beauty. Thou hast been in Eden the garden of God; every precious stone was thy covering, the sardius, topaz, and the diamond, the beryl, the onyx, and the jasper, the*

sapphire, the emerald, and the carbuncle, and gold: the workmanship of thy tabrets and of thy pipes was prepared in thee in the day that thou wast created. Thou art the anointed cherub that covereth; and I have set thee so: thou wast upon the holy mountain of God; thou hast walked up and down in the midst of the stones of fire. Thou wast perfect in thy ways from the day that thou wast created, till iniquity was found in thee."
Ezekiel 28:11-15.

Satan's First Abode:

The first abode of Satan is given in verse 12-14 as being a canopy overshadowing the holy throne of God. This passage reveals three things about Lucifer. First, our God created Satan: he was perfect in form and beauty and wisdom. Satan was the wisest and the most beautiful creation of God.

Second, Satan is described as the anointed cherub that covers. In God's celestial realm, angels are the lowest rank over whom is Michael the Archangel. Above the Angels are the seraphim, having six wings and mentioned in Isaiah and Revelation. The highest rank of created beings are the cherubim, and Satan originally was one of the many cherubs. Ezekiel points out that the Cherubim were the bearers of the Shekinah Glory, and they are the closest to the throne of God.

"While the Angels are before the throne, and the seraphim surround the throne, the cherubim are under it and are responsible for carrying the throne of God. The closer of being is to the throne, the higher the being's rank. The cherubim are the closest to the throne of God, and Satan is a cherub. However, at some point in eternity past, God took this one cherub and anointed or messiahed in him, which made him the arch-cherub and elevating him over other cherubs in power and

authority. With this event, then, Satan was the highest of all created beings, not only in wisdom and beauty but also in power and authority. Therefore he was the anointed cherub that covers. The Hebrew word for covers means the covering roof. He is a canopy over the throne of God. In chapter 1 of Ezekiel, while other cherubim were underneath the throne and were carrying the throne, this particular cherub was the canopy over the throne of God. This one was the most prominent cherub of them all."
Dr. Arnold Fruchtenbaum

In the first part of verse 15, God declared that he was perfect *in your ways from the day in which you were created*. The corruption of Satan and his actions came after his creation, for he was so perfect that he even had the power of contrary choices; to choose contrary to his nature. By nature, he was a holy and perfect being, yet he had the ability to make an unholy and imperfect choice.

Satan's Second Abode:

Sometime after the creation of angelic beings (Job 38:4-7), God created the heavens and the earth (Genesis 1:1). God placed different parts of the universe over to the authority of different angelic beings. The earth was given to the authority of Lucifer (Satan). The garden of Eden, described in Ezekiel 28:13, explains how the entire planet looked when it was initially created. It had no oceans or seas and was covered by the brightness of precious stones mentioned in this verse.

> *"Thou hast been in Eden the garden of God; every precious stone was thy covering, the sardius, topaz, and the diamond, the beryl, the onyx, and the jasper, the sapphire, the emerald, and the carbuncle, and gold: the workmanship of thy tabrets and of thy pipes was prepared in thee in the day that thou wast created. Thou art*

the anointed cherub that covereth; and I have set thee so: thou wast upon the holy mountain of God; thou hast walked up and down in the midst of the stones of fire." Ezekiel 28:13-14.

These same stones appear later in the breastplate of the High Priest. In Satan's case, they acted as a canopy over him. Verse 13 has the words the tabrets and pipes are probably referring to musical instruments used in the worship of God. Satan, before his fall, had specific duties where he served as a priest in heaven. It appears that Satan was the heavenly high priest. Of course, since his fall, he no longer serves in that capacity.

"By the multitude of thy merchandise they have filled the midst of thee with violence, and thou hast sinned: therefore I will cast thee as profane out of the mountain of God: and I will destroy thee, O covering cherub, from the midst of the stones of fire. Thine heart was lifted up because of thy beauty; thou hast corrupted thy wisdom because of thy brightness: I will cast thee to the ground, I will lay thee before kings, that they may behold thee." Ezekiel 28:16-17.

Satan, looking at his wisdom, beauty, power, authority, and meditating on these things, ultimately led to his rise of pride and, thus, Satan's sin. The content of Satan's pride with his declaration of five '*I wills*' is found in Isaiah.

"How art thou fallen from heaven, O Lucifer, son of the morning! How art thou cut down to the ground, which didst weaken the nations! For thou hast said in thine heart, I will ascend into heaven; I will exalt my throne above the

stars of God: <u>I will</u> sit also upon the mount of the congregation, in the sides of the north: <u>I will</u> ascend above the heights of the clouds; <u>I will</u> be like the most High." Isaiah 14:12-14.

Satan's desire for his own will is the basis of all sin in the world. He wanted to be God. Adam and Eve's desire to be their own God was what caused the fall in the garden of Eden. Even now, 6000 years later, we want to be our own gods. Sin arises when we do our own will in opposition to God's will.

Satan's Third Abode:

The third abode of Satan is in our present atmosphere.

"Wherein in time past ye walked according to the course of this world, according to the prince of the power of the air, the spirit that now worketh in the children of disobedience:" Ephesians 2:2.

"For we wrestle not against flesh and blood, but against principalities, against powers, against the rulers of the darkness of this world, against spiritual wickedness in high places." Ephesians 6:12.

Since the deceiving of Adam and Eve in the Garden of Eden, Satan has repeatedly attempted to become the God of this world. I covered many of his attempts in my book (**Look Out: The World Without Christians**). From the temptation of Eve to the crucifixion of Jesus, he has repeatedly attempted to get mankind to worship him and will continue until God casts him into the Lake of Fire.

He still has access to heaven, which allows him to accuse the brethren. He functioned that way in the life of Job and continues to accuse believers today. Satan also has access to the earth. He is now the prince of this world, and ruler of this age, and can offer this world to whomever he wills as he did to Jesus in the wilderness temptation.

He often appears as a roaring lion. Satan has generated all the anti-Semitic campaigns throughout Jewish history as a roaring lion. Satan has inspired persecutions of Christians throughout church history as a roaring lion.

However, he also appears on earth as an angel of light. Satan's primary aim is to deceive. By instigating counterfeit religions that often look like the real worship, he has been able to implement a work of deception even among the true believers, encouraging them to be very experience-oriented. This program of fraud is carried out amongst believers and unbelievers alike. The apostle Paul warns us about this.

> *"But I fear, lest by any means, as the serpent beguiled Eve through his subtilty, so your minds should be corrupted from the simplicity that is in Christ. For if he that cometh preacheth another Jesus, whom we have not preached, or if ye receive another spirit, which ye have not received, or another gospel, which ye have not accepted, ye might well bear with him." 2 Corinthians 11:3-4.*

Paul warned in this passage about another: Jesus, Spirit, Gospel.

> *"For such are false apostles, deceitful workers, transforming themselves into the apostles of Christ. And no marvel; for Satan himself is transformed into an angel of light." 2 Corinthians 11:13-14.*

Those preaching a counterfeit Jesus are false apostles. They sound like real ministers by appearing as an *"angel of light"* but really represents Satan, the Angel of darkness.

> *"Many will say to me in that day, Lord, Lord, have we not prophesied in thy name? and in thy name have cast out devils? and in thy name done many wonderful works? And then will I profess unto them, I never knew you: depart from me, ye that work iniquity." Matthew 7:22-23.*

Today Satan dwells in the atmosphere and has access to heaven as the accuser and access to the earth for the purpose of deceptive destruction or spreading falsehood, He is using a counterfeit program to spread counterfeit ministers of Jesus, preaching a counterfeit Jesus and performing counterfeit signs, miracles, and wonders. Also, as part of his work in his third abode, he uses temptation to usurp authority over the earth by causing man to sin. By causing man to fall, Satan succeeded in keeping man from using the authority God had given him over the earth's creation.

Satan's Fourth Abode:

In the middle of the tribulation, Satan will be cast out of his present abode into the fourth abode and will be confined to this earth for the rest of the Tribulation.

> *"And there was war in heaven: Michael and his angels fought against the dragon; and the dragon fought and his angels, And prevailed not; neither was their place found any more in heaven. And the great dragon was cast out, that old serpent, called the Devil, and Satan, which deceiveth the whole world: he was cast out into*

the earth, and his angels were cast out with him. And I heard a loud voice saying in heaven, Now is come salvation, and strength, and the kingdom of our God, and the power of his Christ: for the accuser of our brethren is cast down, which accused them before our God day and night." Revelation 12:7-10.

Halfway through the tribulation period, Michael, the Archangel, will cast Satan and his demons out of heaven. He will spend the last 3 ½ years of the tribulation attempting to destroy the Jews once and for all, using the false Prophet and the Antichrist to destroy Israel.

Satan's Fifth Abode:

Satan's fifth abode will be in the Abyss, where he will be incarcerated for a thousand years during the Messiah's kingdom. Sin and death in the realm of the Messiah will be significantly reduced, although not eliminated.

"And I saw an angel come down from heaven, having the key of the bottomless pit and a great chain in his hand. And he laid hold on the dragon, that old serpent, which is the Devil, and Satan, and bound him a thousand years, And cast him into the bottomless pit, and shut him up, and set a seal upon him, that he should deceive the nations no more, till the thousand years should be fulfilled: and after that, he must be loosed a little season." Revelation 20:1-3.

During the kingdom of Jesus, the Messiah will fulfill his calling of exercising authority over the created world.

"For unto the angels hath he not put in subjection the world to come, whereof we speak. But one in a certain place testified, saying, What is man, that thou art mindful of him? Or the son of man, that thou visitest him? Thou madest him a little lower than the angels; thou crownedst him with glory and honour, and didst set him over the works of thy hands: Thou hast put all things in subjection under his feet. For in that he put all in subjection under him, he left nothing that is not put under him. But now we see not yet all things put under him. But we see Jesus, who was made a little lower than the angels for the suffering of death, crowned with glory and honour; that he by the grace of God should taste death for every man." Hebrews 2:5-9.

Satan's Sixth Abode:

When the thousand years are finished, Satan will spend eternity in the lake of fire as his sixth and final abode.

"And the devil that deceived them was cast into the lake of fire and brimstone, where the beast and the false prophet are, and shall be tormented day and night for ever and ever." Revelation 20:9-10.

Because of Satan's being cast into the Lake of fire along with all the other fallen angels (demons) and unredeemed humanity, God will remove the two curses on the earth: death (1 Corinthians15:24-26) and the seas (Revelation 21:1).

11

Final Judgments

"And I saw a great white throne, and him that sat on it, from whose face the earth and the heaven fled away; and there was found no place for them. And I saw the dead, small and great, stand before God; and the books were opened: and another book was opened, which is the book of life: and the dead were judged out of those things which were written in the books, according to their works." Revelation 20:11-12.

"Rev 20:7-10: And when the thousand years are expired, Satan shall be loosed out of his prison, And shall go out to deceive the nations which are in the four quarters of the earth, Gog, and Magog [Gog and Magog in this verse does not refer to another physical battle with Turkey and the Islam confederation as in Ezek 38-39. It is used as a figure of speech in the same sense as when we say e.g., "They will meet their Waterloo." It will be a spiritual battle as there will be no weapons during the

Millennium] to gather them together to battle: the number of whom is as the sand of the sea. And they went up on the breadth of the earth, and compassed the camp of the saints about, and the beloved city: and fire came down from God out of heaven, and devoured them. And the devil that deceived them was cast into the lake of fire and brimstone, where the beast and the false prophet are, and shall be tormented day and night for ever and ever." Prof (Dr) WA. Liebenberg.

Again, he will do the work of deception among all the nations of the Gentiles on earth. By this time, because of a thousand years of human births, there will be many unbelievers. The reference here to Gog and Magog shows that the deception will be a worldwide rebellion and invasion of Israel. These deceived Gentile armies will surround the millennial Jerusalem.

Once those armies arrive at the mountain of Jehovah's house, they will be quickly dispensed with fire out of heaven, destroying them completely and suddenly. God will place the instigator of this revolt in his sixth and final abode. There he will join the Antichrist and the False Prophet, who have been there a thousand years already for an eternity of suffering in the lake of fire.

"It should be remembered that death will still exist in the kingdom. It is only after Satan's final revolt and his confinement in the lake of fire that death can be abolished. It is Satan who caused death for man by tempting the first parents. It is only when the originator of death for man is forever confined in his final abode that death could be abolished. And at this point, it will be. With this, the millennial kingdom will come to an end. All things will now have been placed in total subjection to the Messiah, and that totality of subjection will now be subjugated to God the Father in order that God may be all in all." Dr. Arnold Fruchtenbaum.

The Great White Throne Judgment:

To prepare for the establishment of the eternal order that we call Heaven will be the last judgment of God's creation.

> *"And I saw a great white throne, and him that sat on it, from whose face the earth and the heaven fled away; and there was found no place for them. And I saw the dead, small and great, stand before God; and the books were opened: and another book was opened, which is the book of life: and the dead were judged out of those things which were written in the books," Revelation 20:11-12.*

The one sitting on the throne in John's vision is Jesus, the Messiah, for it is to him that God has given all judgment.

> *"For the Father judgeth no man, but hath committed all judgment unto the Son." John 5:22.*

At the end of the final rebellion will be the second resurrection. The first resurrection will be composed of believers only, and the second resurrection will be of unbelievers only. God will reunite the bodies of all unbelievers with all the souls relinquished by hell. They will then be judged at the Great White throne.

This judgment will be the judgment all unbelievers of all time. The purpose of the judgment is to determine the degrees of punishment based upon degrees of sinfulness and the amount of the knowledge of God and their response to it.

"One's appearance at this particular judgment will be a direct result of failing to believe in Jesus as Savior. However, the degree of punishment will be based on one's works. In determining the degrees of punishment, books are mentioned in addition to the Book of Life. The Book of Life referenced in verse 12 contains the names of every person

who has ever been born. Those who believe in Jesus have their names retained in the book of life, according to Revelation 3:5. However, the unsaved have their names blotted out the book of life:" Dr. Arnold Fruchtenbaum.

> **"Let them be blotted out of the book of the living, and not be written with the righteous."**
> **Psalm 69:28.**

If their names are not found in the Book of Life, they will show as unsaved and worthy of eternal judgment. Those whose names are found are the ones whose sins of all been forgiven based upon their faith in the finished work of Christ on the cross.

The other books mentioned in verse 12 contain one's deeds and responses to God's offers of salvation. It is based on what's written in these books that determine the degrees of punishment each person shall receive.

The Lake of Fire:

> *"And I saw the dead, small and great, stand before God; and the books were opened: and another book was opened, which is the book of life: and the dead were judged out of those things which were written in the books, according to their works. And the sea gave up the dead which were in it; and death and hell delivered up the dead which were in them: and they were judged every man according to their works. And death and hell were cast into the lake of fire. This is the second death. And whosoever was not found written in the book of life, was cast into the lake of fire." Revelation 20:12-15.*

In the Old Testament times, all who died went to a place called in Hebrew, *Sheol*, and in the Greek *Hades*. While the Old Testament sacrifices covered their sins, only the death of the Messiah/Jesus could remove their sins. This place had two compartments, as is described in Luke's passage concerning the rich man and Lazarus (Luke 16:19-31). One chamber was called *hell* and was a place of torment. The other compartment for the righteous was known as *Abraham's bosom or paradise; it was a place of comfort* for those looking for God's saviour, but it was not heaven.

"When Jesus died, he not only paid the price for all future sins, but he also paid the price for all previous sins (Romans 3:25; Hebrews 9:15). Thus, the sins of the Old Testament saints were removed. What happened next recorded in Ephesians 4:8-10:" Dr. Arnold Fruchtenbaum.

"Wherefore he saith, When he ascended up on high, he led captivity captive, and gave gifts unto men. (Now that he ascended, what is it but that he also descended first into the lower parts of the earth? He that descended is the same also that ascended up far above all heavens, that he might fill all things.)" Ephesians 4:8-10.

"While His body remained in the tomb, His soul went down into paradise side of Sheol, or Hades, announcing that the atonement had been made. At the time of His ascension, all the souls of the Old Testament saints were removed out of Abraham's Bosom, or Paradise, and brought into heaven. In this way, the righteous portion of Sheol or Hades was eliminated and is no longer in existence." Dr. Arnold Fruchtenbaum.

So today, when an unbeliever dies, and his body is buried, his soul goes to Hell. However, when a believer dies, and his body is buried, his soul and spirit go immediately to Paradise in the third heaven, where Jesus and God are preparing a place for them.

"We are confident, I say, and willing rather to be absent from the body, and to be present with the Lord. Wherefore we labour, that, whether present or absent, we may be accepted of him." 2 Corinthians 5:8-9.

"All those on whom this judgement is meted are consigned to the Lake of Fire forever. This Great White Throne judgement may rightly be called the 'final judgement.' It constitutes the termination of HaShem's resurrection and judgement program. The time of the judgement—it is clearly indicated that this judgment takes place after the expiration of the Messianic Age reign of Yeshua. The place of the judgement—unknown. The basis of judgement—that there will be degrees of judgement/punishment meted out to the unsaved is suggested from Scripture (Luke 12:47-48). But the sentence to the second death will be passed on all." Prof. (Dr.) WA. Liebenberg.

Part Three

Eternal Heaven Our
Eternal Home

12

All Things New

"And I saw a new heaven and a new earth: for the first heaven and the first earth were passed away; and there was no more sea." Revelation 21:1.

The Eternal Order is the prime point of the New Testament prophecies. Old Testament prophecies dealt with the Messianic Kingdom. The only information the Bible gives for the Eternal Order is found in the last two chapters of Revelation.

The millennial kingdom only lasted 1,000 years. But the promises made to David were of an eternal Throne. Jesus will continue his position of authority on the Davidic Throne into the Eternal Order.

To prepare for the Great White Throne judgment, the old heavens and earth were destroyed.

"To replace the old order, new heavens and a new earth will be created. A significant element missing on the new earth is the sea." Dr. Arnold Fruchtenbaum.

"Here is the explanation by world-renowned scientists, the late

Dr. Henry Morris: 'there will be, in fact, no need for a Sea on the new earth. The presidency is needed for a reservoir for the maintenance of the hydrologic cycle.... In the new earth, all men and women who live there will have their glorified bodies with no more need of water. The resurrected bodies will be composed, like that of the Lord Jesus, of flesh and bone but apparently with no need for blood to serve as a cleanser and restore of the bodies flesh as it is at present. This, in turn, eliminates the major need for water on the earth (the blood is 90% water, and present-day human flesh is about 65% water).'" Dr. David Jeremiah.

The ecology of the new earth will differ from our present planet. There is a freshwater river flowing from the throne of God, watering the trees of life growing on its shores.

"The seas that were created in Genesis 1: 2 will be put back into heaven and in the center of the earth, where they originated. The earth will be 'renewed to its original state as before the fall of Lucifer and before the first rebellion of the earth against God.' The world's new water source will come from the rivers, lakes, and small seas." John Hagee.

Since salt is a preservative, and there will be no decay in heaven, no salt will be needed for the preservation of anything.

Formerly the earth comprised a mineral garden, covered with precious stones, and it served as Satan's second abode:

> **"Moreover the word of the LORD came unto me, saying, Son of man, take up a lamentation upon the king of Tyrus** (Satan)**, and say unto him, Thus saith the Lord GOD; Thou sealest up the sum, full of wisdom, and perfect in beauty. Thou hast been in Eden the garden of God; every precious stone was thy covering, the sardius, topaz, and the diamond, the beryl, the onyx, and the jasper, the sapphire, the emerald, and the carbuncle, and gold: the workmanship of thy tabrets and of thy pipes was prepared in thee in the day that thou wast created. Thou art the anointed cherub that**

*covereth; and I have set thee so: thou wast upon
the holy mountain of God; thou hast walked up
and down in the midst of the stones of fire. Thou
wast perfect in thy ways from the day that thou
wast created, till iniquity was found in thee. By
the multitude of thy merchandise they have filled
the midst of thee with violence, and thou hast
sinned: therefore I will cast thee as profane out
of the mountain of God: and I will destroy thee,
O covering cherub, from the midst of the stones
of fire." Ezekiel 28:11-16.*

However, when Satan fell, everything under his authority was
judged along with him. This judgment included dissolving the
earth's elements in the waters. Just as when Adam and Eve were
created, the earth was empty, without shape and dark.

*"And the earth was without form, and void; and
darkness was upon the face of the deep. And the
Spirit of God moved upon the face of the waters."
Genesis 1:2.*

The New Jerusalem, where Jesus will rule over the new earth,
and the new heavens will not be created new because it will come
down from heaven and will be as a bride adorned for her marriage
ceremony. The apostle Paul described the new Jerusalem as that
which is free:

*"But Jerusalem which is above is free, which is
the mother of us all." Galatians 4:26.*

This is the city that Abraham was seeking.

"By faith he sojourned in the land of promise, as in a strange country, dwelling in tabernacles with Isaac and Jacob, the heirs with him of the same promise: For he looked for a city which hath foundations, whose builder and maker is God." Hebrews 11:9-10.

Hebrews describes it as the eternal dwelling place of the saved.

"But ye are come unto mount Sion, and unto the city of the living God, the heavenly Jerusalem, and to an innumerable company of angels, To the general assembly and church of the firstborn, which are written in heaven, and to God the Judge of all, and to the spirits of just men made perfect, And to Jesus the mediator of the new covenant, and to the blood of sprinkling, that speaketh better things than that of Abel. See that ye refuse not him that speaketh. For if they escaped not who refused him that spake on earth, much more shall not we escape, if we turn away from him that speaketh from heaven:" Hebrews 12:22-25.

The triune God will inhabit the New Jerusalem, along with all the angelic host, the church saints, the Old Testament saints, the tribulation saints, and lastly, the millennial saints.

"And I heard a great voice out of heaven saying, Behold, the tabernacle of God is with men, and he will dwell with them, and they shall be his people, and God himself shall be with them, and be their God." Revelation 21:3.

Jerusalem, under the old order, suffered constant subjugation by various forces, but the New Eternal Jerusalem has been eternally free and always will be. It will come down from heaven and be joined to Israel on the new earth. And God will dwell *(tabernacle)* with man forever. *Tabernacled* is a reference to the Shekinah glory of God abiding with men as it once did in wilderness tabernacle and Solomon's Temple.

Eternal New Jerusalem:

This city is the Eternal City that houses the Eternal Temple, where Jesus applied His sinless blood of atonement on the altar.

> *"But Christ being come an high priest of good things to come, by a greater and more perfect tabernacle, not made with hands, that is to say, not of this building; Neither by the blood of goats and calves, but by his own blood he entered in once into the holy place, having obtained eternal redemption for us." Hebrews 9:11-12.*

The Eternal Temple will be the ultimate resting place of God's *Shekinah* Glory. It abode with man in the tabernacle until Israel sought after other gods. The glory returned to dwell in the temple built by Solomon. But later, Ezekiel records Shekinah Glory leaving the temple and the city of Jerusalem to return to heaven.

> *"Behold, your house is left unto you desolate. For I say unto you, Ye shall not see me henceforth, till ye shall say, Blessed is he that cometh in the name of the Lord." Matthew 23:38-39.*

The glorified Jesus, at the end of His ministry, brought the glory back to the Temple in His day, but he was rejected and therefore left the Temple of God empty.

The City of God:

John described the city of God that he saw:

> *"And had a wall great and high, and had twelve gates, and at the gates twelve angels, and names written thereon, which are the names of the twelve tribes of the children of Israel: On the east three gates; on the north three gates; on the south three gates; and on the west three gates." Revelation 21:12-13.*

The Bible says the wall of Eternal Jerusalem to be great and high, emphasizing its protection. The wall will have twelve gates, three on each side, each under the authority of an angel, and named for the twelve tribes of Israel.

> *"And the wall of the city had twelve foundations, and in them the names of the twelve apostles of the Lamb." Revelation 21:14.*

John refers to the foundations of the wall. I don't know whether he is referring to the sections between the twelve gates or if he is referring to stacked portions of the foundation, which would create a beautiful rainbow. However, each of the Lord's apostles has a section of the wall named for them just as the tribes of Israel are memorialized with the gates; the apostles will be memorialized with the eternal foundations.

> *"And he that talked with me had a golden reed to measure the city, and the gates thereof, and*

*the wall thereof. And the city lieth foursquare,
and the length is as large as the breadth: and he
measured the city with the reed, twelve thousand
furlongs. The length and the breadth and the
height of it are equal. And he measured the wall
thereof, an hundred and forty and four cubits,
according to the measure of a man, that is, of the
angel." Revelation 21:15-17.*

The city appears to be shaped like a cube with the four sides and the height all being equal measurements of 12,000 furlongs (approximately 1,500 miles). If you were to place the size of the city in the United States, the footprint would cover the entire eastern half of the country. The entire city is constructed of transparent gold.

The height of the city could accommodate buildings having 792,000 floors. The wall surrounding the city will measure 216 feet high.

The foundations of the wall Around the Eternal Jerusalem is composed of different precious stones. The Bible shows the following dominant colors of each stone.

1—Jasper—Green
2—Sapphire—Blue
3—Chalcedony—Greenish
4—Emerald--- Green
5—Sardonyx --- Red and white
6—Sardius--- Fiery red
7—Chrysolite--- Golden yellow
8—Beryl --- Aqua green
9—Topaz --- Greenish-yellow
10—Cheysoprase --- Golden green
11—Jacinth --- Violet
12—Amethyst --- Purple

According to Ezekiel 28:13, the first earth before Satan's fall had ten precious gemstones.

> *"-- the sardius, topaz, and the diamond, the beryl, the onyx, and the jasper, the sapphire, the emerald, and the carbuncle, and gold--"*
> *Ezekiel 28:13.*

The new earth will enjoy all the perfections of the first earth along with the addition of two additional stones.

Each gate is made of a single colossal pearl, and the streets themselves are composed of transparent gold.

> *"And I saw no temple therein: for the Lord God Almighty, and the Lamb are the temple of it. And the city had no need of the sun, neither of the moon, to shine in it: for the glory of God did lighten it, and the Lamb is the light thereof. And the nations of them which are saved shall walk in the light of it: and the kings of the earth do bring their glory and honour into it."*
> *Revelation 21:22-24.*

Besides the New Earth not having any seas, the Eternal Jerusalem will not have a temple. Since the triune God will inhabit the city along with the redeemed of all ages, there will be no need for a sacrificial meeting place. There is also no need of a sun in a moon in the new heavens. The purpose of the sun and the moon in our earth is mainly to track the passage of days and control the tides. In Eternal Jerusalem, everything is infinite. The need for the Sun is also done away with as the New Jerusalem, and the Shekinah glory of God will illuminate the new earth.

"And the gates of it shall not be shut at all by day: for there shall be no night there. And they shall bring the glory and honour of the nations into it. And there shall in no wise enter into it any thing that defileth, neither whatsoever worketh abomination, or maketh a lie: but they which are written in the Lamb's book of life." Revelation 21:25-27.

Twelve angels maintain the twelve pearly gates surrounding the city, and they are never closed. All those whose names are written in the Lamb's Book of Life will have free access into the city, and nothing unrighteous will ever be allowed to enter the eternal city. All the unrighteousness will be confined to the lake of fire.

John next describes the river of life, which flows out of the throne of God and the Messiah. It is a river of crystal brightness throughout the city of New Jerusalem. Along its banks is the tree of life.

"And he shewed me a pure river of water of life, clear as crystal, proceeding out of the throne of God and of the Lamb. In the midst of the street of it, and on either side of the river, was there the tree of life, which bare twelve manner of fruits, and yielded her fruit every month: and the leaves of the tree were for the healing of the nations." Revelation 22:1.

"The tree of life that existed in the Garden of Eden (Gen. 2:9, 3:22, 24) will now return. The trunk of the tree will extend to both sides of the eternal river of life and will be characterized by its productivity, bearing fresh fruit each month of the year. It should be noted that the word month is used, so some kind of dating system will be present in the eternal order. Since there will be no sun, moon, or night, it will be radically

different dating system than the one which we presently live. But there will be a dating system of some kind. The leaves of the Tree of life are for the healing of the nations. The Greek word translated healing is the source of the modern English word "therapeutic." The purpose of the leaves is not to heal the existing sickness, for they will not exist to the eternal Order; rather: they will be a health-giving to the nations. There will be no sickness in the Eternal Order because of the leaves of the tree of life. The Greek word for nations is a term used that means Gentiles. This again shows that the Jewish-Gentile distinction continues through eternity. There is, therefore, no functional difference." Dr. Arnold Fruchtenbaum.

Occupants of the eternal order are free from the curse in Genesis chapter three. The residents will include the Lamb and all the redeemed of all ages. The presence of the Shekinah Glory fills the Eternal Order. God himself will provide all necessary illumination forever.

> **"And there shall be no more curse: but the throne of God and of the Lamb shall be in it; and his servants shall serve him: And they shall see his face; and his name shall be in their foreheads. And there shall be no night there; and they need no candle, neither light of the sun; for the Lord God giveth them light: and they shall reign for ever and ever." Revelation 22:3-5.**

13

We Will See God

*"And he said, I beseech thee, shew me thy glory.
And he (God) said, I will make all my goodness
pass before thee, and I will proclaim the name
of the LORD before thee; and will be gracious
to whom I will be gracious, and will shew mercy
on whom I will shew mercy. And he said, Thou
canst not see my face: for there shall no man see
me, and live." Exodus 33:18-20.*

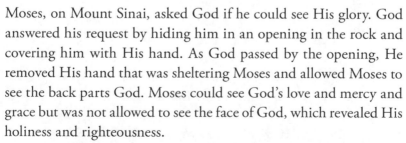

Moses, on Mount Sinai, asked God if he could see His glory. God answered his request by hiding him in an opening in the rock and covering him with His hand. As God passed by the opening, He removed His hand that was sheltering Moses and allowed Moses to see the back parts God. Moses could see God's love and mercy and grace but was not allowed to see the face of God, which revealed His holiness and righteousness.

"The Bible tells us that no one has ever seen God (John 1:18) except

the Lord Jesus Christ. In Exodus 33:20, God declares, **"You cannot see my face, for no one may see me and live."** *These Scriptures seem to contradict other Scriptures which describe various people "seeing" God. For example, Exodus 33:11 describes Moses speaking to God "face to face." How could Moses speak with God "face to face" if no one can see God's face and live? In this instance, the phrase "face to face" is a figure of speech indicating they were in very close communion. God and Moses were speaking to each other as if they were two human beings having a close conversation."* www.Gotquestions.org.

The Bible describes many times when God has appeared in the form of a man or an angel, often called the "Angel of the Lord," to various individuals.

> **"And Jacob called the name of the place Peniel: for I have seen God face to face, and my life is preserved." Genesis 32:30.**

Jacob saw God appearing as a man; he even wrestled with God, but he did not truly see the glorified God.

> **"And Manoah said unto his wife, We shall surely die, because we have seen God." Judges 13:22.**

Samson's parents were terrified when they realized they received the prophecy concerning Sampson directly from God, but they had only seen Him appearing as an angel.

Jesus was God in the flesh (John 1:1, 14), so when people saw Him, they were seeing God.

> **"In the beginning was the Word, and the Word was with God, and the Word was God." John 1:1.**

> **"And the Word was made flesh, and dwelt among us, (and we beheld his glory, the glory as of the**

only begotten of the Father,) full of grace and truth." John 1:14.

So, yes, God can be "seen," and many people have "seen" God. No one has ever seen God revealed in all His glory. In our fallen human condition, if God were to reveal Himself to us fully, we would be consumed by his holiness. A sinful person cannot see the holiness of God face to face without the sanctifying blood of Jesus in between.

Therefore, God veils Himself and appears in forms in which we can "see" Him. However, this differs from seeing God with all His glory and holiness displayed. People have seen visions of God, images of God, and appearances of God, but no one has ever seen God in all His fullness.

> *"And he said, I will make all my goodness pass before thee, and I will proclaim the name of the LORD before thee; and will be gracious to whom I will be gracious, and will shew mercy on whom I will shew mercy. And he said, Thou canst not see my face: for there shall no man see me, and live." Exodus 33:19-20.*

Job prophesied of the day when he would physically in the flesh see God. All the redeemed of all time, once they have received glorified bodies, will be able to see holy God's fullness with the Shekinah glory. Once we have our glorified sinless bodies, we will see God in the Eternal Heaven.

> *"For I know that my redeemer liveth, and that he shall stand at the latter day upon the earth: And though after my skin worms destroy this body, yet in my flesh shall I see God: Whom I shall see for myself, and mine eyes shall behold, and not*

another; though my reins be consumed within
me. But ye should say, Why persecute we him,
seeing the root of the matter is found in me?"
Job 19:25-28.

There will be no sin to separate us from God's Holiness and righteousness, and we will see Jehovah as *abba father* (*daddy*).

I am:

"In the beginning was the Word, and the Word
was with God, and the Word was God." John 1:1.

The apostle John tells us that the Word, Jesus, not only dwelt with God from the beginning but is God. Jesus is the son of God. When God called Moses to go back to Egypt and lead God's people, Israel, out of slavery, Moses asked God 'whom shall I say sent me.' God told Moses his name was '*I Am that I Am*.' I Am means the God who is eternally present. Jesus said to the Pharisees '*before Abraham was, I am.*' And when He was arrested on the Mount of Olives, and the soldiers ask his name, he replied to them *I am* He, and they all got knocked off their feet at the power of His name. Throughout the Gospels that he was the incarnate deity, the creator of the heavens and earth.

"And Moses said unto God, Behold, when I come
unto the children of Israel, and shall say unto
them, The God of your fathers hath sent me unto
you; and they shall say to me, What is his name?
What shall I say unto them? [14] *And God said unto*
Moses, I AM THAT I AM: and he said, Thus shalt
thou say unto the children of Israel, I AM hath
sent me unto you." Exodus 3:13.

"I am" means Eternal Presence, **"Yahweh."**

Hebrew-haòyaòh Greek- *aw-yaw'*

The primitive root meaning; *to exist, that is, be* or *become, come to pass.*

In the Midrash, the Hebrew scholars explain this as an active manifestation of the divine existence. God is engaged in the affairs of His world and people. The Midrash states: *"Although He has not displayed His power towards you, He will do so. He is eternal and will certainly redeem you."*

> *"And God said moreover unto Moses, Thus shalt thou say unto the children of Israel, The LORD God of your fathers, the God of Abraham, the God of Isaac, and the God of Jacob, hath sent me unto you: this is my name for ever, and this is my memorial unto all generations." Exodus 3:15.*

LORD here is the translation of the Divine Name written in four Hebrew Letters Y H W H. It gives expression to the fact that He was, He is and that He will be forever. This name stresses the loving-kindness and faithfulness of God to His creatures.

> *"And God spake unto Moses, and said unto him, I am the LORD: And I appeared unto Abraham, unto Isaac, and unto Jacob, by the name of God Almighty, but by my name JEHOVAH was I not known to them." Exodus 6:2-3.*

Jehovah - *(the) self Existent or eternal*; Jehovah is the Jewish national name of God:—Jehovah, the Lord.

Once we are in the Eternal Heaven, we will see Jehovah face to face and communicate with him directly without fear.

14

Our Life After Death

"And I knew such a man, (whether in the body, or out of the body, I cannot tell: God knoweth;) How that he was caught up into paradise, and heard unspeakable words, which it is not lawful for a man to utter." 2 Corinthians 12:3-4

Paradise is mentioned only three times in the Scriptures. The first is when Jesus promised the dying thief on the cross that he would be with him in Paradise.

> *"And he said unto Jesus, Lord, remember me when thou comest into thy kingdom. And Jesus said unto him, Verily I say unto thee, To day shalt thou be with me in paradise." Luke 23:42-43.*

The second time is when Paul was caught up into Paradise.

Jim Zeigler

> *"How that he was caught up into paradise, and heard unspeakable words, which it is not lawful for a man to utter. Of such an one will I glory: yet of myself I will not glory, but in mine infirmities."*
> *2 Corinthians 12:4-5.*

The third mention is when John gives us a description of the overcoming saints who will eat of the tree of life in Paradise.

> *"He that hath an ear, let him hear what the Spirit saith unto the churches; To him that overcometh will I give to eat of the tree of life, which is in the midst of the paradise of God." Revelation 2:7.*

When Jesus died, and while his body was in the tomb, his spirit descended into the center of the earth to Paradise, where Lazarus the beggar was. There Jesus preached his redemption to the Old Testament believers who were looking for his coming as Messiah. The Bible tells us He took all the people in Paradise with him to the Third Heaven. While in heaven, Jesus applied his sinless blood, shed on the cross at Calvary, upon the sacrificial altar in heaven. Then he rose from the dead and appeared to his disciples and other believers for the forty days before he ascended into the clouds.

Visitors to Heaven:

There have been published descriptions of the Third Heaven, from individuals who have had near-death experiences. And there are thousands of them recorded, many of which do not conform with biblical principles.

However, there are many, especially in these last days, which come from very reliable sources and do not contradict Scripture. It's through these accounts that we can get a glimpse of what is waiting for us in the Eternal Heaven.

Perry Stone, in his book "Secrets of the Third Heaven," tells of one such experience his father Fred had:

"When my father, Fred Stone, was called into the ministry in his late teens, he was blessed with a remarkable spiritual experience in which he saw the very edge of the third heaven. Somewhere beyond was the abode where the souls of the righteous dwell. He said, 'while sitting in a white cane back chair, I felt a surge in my heart and suddenly slumped over. I thought I had a heart attack and had died. Immediately, my soul came out of my body, like taking a hand out of a glove. My soul (or spirit) was suddenly whisked through space so fast that I was in a fetal position, and could feel the pressure of my assent. When I stopped, I opened my eyes, and I was standing in an open space on absolutely nothing. I was surrounded by the most beautiful, deep blue color, unlike anything I have seen on earth. The blue skies on earth pale in comparison to the rich, deep blue color surrounding the edge of heaven.'"

Other accounts that I have read always referred to the sky as a deep blue color not seen on planet Earth. All the colors in heaven are far more vibrant and brilliant than we see here today. As humans living on earth, we all have five senses, but in heaven, God will multiply the five senses with higher intensity. Colors, smells, and sounds will be of a higher dimension in the spiritual realm.

Many men and women who have had a near-death experience tell of the fantastic ability to communicate through thoughts and not words. It's as if each person can read the thoughts of another person near to them with no verbal communication. Jesus could perceive the thoughts of those around him, as recorded in Matthew and Luke. According to Hebrews, God can discern the thoughts and intents of the heart.

"For the word of God is quick, and powerful, and sharper than any two-edged sword, piercing even to the dividing asunder of soul and spirit, and of

the joints and marrow, and is a discerner of the thoughts and intents of the heart." Hebrews 4:12.

All these people claim a sense of peace so intense that they do not want to return to their lives on earth. According to first-hand reports, when a Christian dies having a clear mental awareness, they often see loved ones. They appear in their room or place of death to tell them it is time to come home with them. They die in peace in the room that is, for a moment, filled with certain electricity, creating an almost holy atmosphere.

But when a nonbeliever dies, many often die screaming about a fire at their feet, moving up their legs and seeing some horrible creatures.

"Testimonies of thousands of near-death moments indicate that a few seconds prior to death, many people who are drug-induced or in semi-covert conditions suddenly open their eyes and have a keen awareness not just of their surroundings and the family in the room, but their eyes are opened into another realm that their family members in the room do not see." Perry Stone.

A new name:

The book of Revelation informs us that believers of every age when they arrive in heaven after the Rapture or Resurrection will receive a new name.

> **"He that hath an ear, let him hear what the Spirit saith unto the churches; To him that overcometh will I give to eat of the hidden manna, and will give him a white stone, and in the stone a new name written, which no man knoweth saving he that receiveth it." Revelation 2:17.**

A white stone was given to the defendant in the Roman courts as a verdict of innocence. Bible scholars believe that this name is the original name God assigned to us when we were formed in the womb. God himself gave us the name different from everyone else's name.

"Before I formed thee in the belly, I knew thee..."
Jeremiah 1:5.

Many people see spouses and family and friends during their brief visit to the third heaven. Those they see look as though they're in their early 30s, but some are older, and some are even younger, even children. Some appear much older. When John saw Christ in his apocalyptic vision, Christ had white hair. That may explain why, after his resurrection, Mary does not recognize Jesus, who thought he was the gardener.

15

Heavenly Neighbors

"And I beheld, and I heard the voice of many angels round about the throne and the beasts and the elders: and the number of them was ten thousand times ten thousand, and thousands of thousands; Saying with a loud voice, Worthy is the Lamb that was slain to receive power, and riches, and wisdom, and strength, and honour, and glory, and blessing. And every creature which is in heaven, and on the earth, and under the earth, and such as are in the sea, and all that are in them, heard I saying, Blessing, and honour, and glory, and power, be unto Him that sitteth upon the throne, and unto the Lamb for ever and ever." Revelation 5:11-13.

In Heaven, we will dwell with glorified humans, Angels, and other celestial beings created by God.

Believers will all speak the same language:

There are two types of languages, earthly and heavenly. The apostle Paul said:

> *"Though I speak with the tongues of men and of angels..." 1 Corinthians 13:1.*

From the creation of Adam until the Tower of Babel, about 2,246 years later, all men spoke the same language. It was ar Babel that God divided man's one speech into seventy. Each language then became a nation, as are listed in Genesis chapter ten. It's interesting to note that when Jesus sent out his disciples, he sent seventy.

God's image Makers:

> *"And God said, Let us make man in our image, after our likeness: and let them have dominion over the fish of the sea, and over the fowl of the air, and over the cattle, and over all the earth, and over every creeping thing that creepeth upon the earth." Genesis 1:26.*

"In Genesis 1:26, God says, 'Let us make humankind in our image,' God announces his intention to a group. Who's he talking to? His heavenly host—his council. He's not talking to the other members of the Trinity, because God can't know something they don't! And here the group he's addressing learns what God has decided to do. A better translation of Genesis 1:26 would be that God created humans as his image. To be human is to be God's imager. We are God's representatives, so to speak. The image of God isn't an ability given to us by God, like intelligence. We can lose abilities, but we cannot lose the status of being God's imager." Michael S. Heiser.

We will always be God's imagers, which is why Human life is

so sacred. God shares His authority with humans on Earth. God is the king of all things visible and invisible. He rules. He shares that rule with his family in the spiritual world and the human world.

"*The idea of God wanting us to join his divine family, to be part of his council and live in his presence, helps us understand some amazing things the Bible says. It explains why the Bible refers to believers as "sons of God" or "children of God" (John 1:12; 11:52; Gal. 3:26; 1 John 3:1–3). It explains why believers are described as being "adopted" into God's family (Gal. 4:5–6; Rom. 8:14–6). It explains why we are said to be "heirs" of God and his kingdom (Gal. 4:7; Titus 3:7; James 2:5) and "partakers of the divine nature" (2 Pet. 1:4; see also 1 John 3:2). It explains why, after Jesus returns, he says he will grant believers "to eat of the tree of life, which is in the paradise of God" (Rev. 2:7). It explains why he's promised to share the rule of the nations with us (Rev. 2:26–28), even his own throne (Rev. 3:21). We move forward through this life back to Eden. Heaven"* Michael S. Heiser.

God created us to take part in His plan to make the world all he desires, so that we may enjoy it with him. Jesus is the ultimate example of representing God. In Colossians 1:15, He is called the image of the invisible God. We are to imitate Jesus for that reason.

> **"Who is the image of the invisible God, the firstborn of every creature: For by him were all things created, that are in heaven, and that are in earth, visible and invisible, whether they be thrones, or dominions, or principalities, or powers: all things were created by him, and for him:" Colossians 1:15-16.**

Jim Zeigler

Two Councils, One Destiny:

"Humans are basically God's administration—his council—on earth. We were made to live in God's presence, with his heavenly family. We were made to enjoy him and serve him forever." Michael S. Heiser.

Eden was where heaven and earth intersected. God and his heavenly council members were to occupy the same space as humans, thus uniting the seen and unseen family of God.

God told Adam and Eve, **"Be fruitful and multiply and fill the earth and subdue it, and have dominion... over every living thing that moves on the earth."** This was the task for God's imagers. They would serve God as administrators of His creation. their job was to reproduce and populate the earth and extend Eden to the entire planet.

Adam and Eve failed. Humanity sinned. Earth would have been gradually transformed into a global Eden. We would have had everlasting life on a perfected planet, living with God and his spiritual family.

> **"Wherefore, as by one man sin entered into the world, and death by sin; and so death passed upon all men, for that all have sinned:" Romans 5:12.**

"God loved humanity, so he forgave Adam and Eve. But the rest of humanity from that point on was destined to follow in Adam and Eve's footsteps. We all sin and deserve death without God's intervention (Rom. 6:23). We are mortal and, therefore, sinners. We need salvation." Michael S. Heiser.

In Heaven, we will live with all of God's created beings, animal, human, and spiritual in perfect harmony.

Millions of Angels:

Angels are spiritual beings that may take on human form to complete their role as messengers of God. The Hebrew word in the Old Testament (*mal'ak*) means 'to dispatch as a deputy, ambassador or messenger.' Angels intervene to protect men, women, and children from harm. Often angels have intervened to protect us unawares. Only in heaven will God reveal how many assaults and accidents have been prevented by the supernatural actions of these angelic beings.

The Bible also refers to them as sons of the mighty, sons of God, the congregation of the Mighty, heavenly hosts, and spirits. Each of the innumerable band of angels has a name, but Scripture only discloses the names of five: Satan, the fallen angel; Apollyon, another fallen angel called "the destroyer" by John in Revelation; Michael, the archangel and Gabriel who appeared to Daniel and who announced the births of Jesus and John the Baptist; Palomi, "the numbered" who is named in the original language of the book of Daniel, and tells Daniel how long it will be before Christ comes to cleanse the defiled earthly sanctuary.

They are invisible to humans, but they sometimes become visible as needed to accomplish their God-sent missions. Balaam's donkey saw the angel blocking the way, even though Balaam did not.

"They usually take on human form as they deliver messages from God and minister to people. Various places in Scripture tell about their physical features, including heads, faces, eyes, mouth, hair, hands, and feet. Angels have emotions, appetite, passions, desires, willpower, language, intelligence, knowledge, and wisdom. They also have patience, meekness, and modesty. The Bible says the angels who serve God are holy." Grant R. Jeffries.

Angels have many responsibilities in God's government. They not only minister to men, but they also execute the judgments of God and rule the nations. They are not the pacifist angels of medieval art or greeting cards, but they wage war against God's enemies.

> *"For we wrestle not against flesh and blood,*
> *but against principalities, against powers,*
> *against the rulers of the darkness of this world,*
> *against spiritual wickedness in high places."*
> *Ephesians 6:12.*

The millions of millions of angels will guard the gates of Jerusalem to prevent anything unholy from entering. They will ride on heavenly horses with Jesus in the campaign of Armageddon as He conquers the world and sets up His Eternal Kingdom.

> *"And I saw heaven opened, and behold a white*
> *horse; and he that sat upon him was called*
> *Faithful and True, and in righteousness he doth*
> *judge and make war. His eyes were as a flame*
> *of fire, and on his head were many crowns; and*
> *he had a name written, that no man knew, but*
> *he himself. And he was clothed with a vesture*
> *dipped in blood: and his name is called The Word*
> *of God. And the armies which were in heaven*
> *followed him upon white horses, clothed in fine*
> *linen, white and clean." Revelation 19:11-14.*

Cherubim:

> *"And before the throne there was a sea of glass*
> *like unto crystal: and in the midst of the throne,*
> *and round about the throne, were four beasts*
> *full of eyes before and behind. And the first beast*
> *was like a lion, and the second beast like a calf,*
> *and the third beast had a face as a man, and the*
> *fourth beast was like a flying eagle. And the four*

beasts had each of them six wings about him; and they were full of eyes within: and they rest not day and night, saying, Holy, holy, holy, Lord God Almighty, which was, and is, and is to come. And when those beasts give glory and honour and thanks to him that sat on the throne, who liveth for ever and ever," Revelation 4:6-9.

The cherubim magnify the holiness and power of God. They also serve as a visible reminder of the majesty and glory of God and His abiding presence with His people. God created Lucifer as a Cherub but he fell because of his pride and wanting to replace God and became known as Satan.

Seraphim:

"Above it stood the seraphims: each one had six wings; with twain he covered his face, and with twain he covered his feet, and with twain he did fly. And one cried unto another, and said, Holy, holy, holy, is the LORD of hosts: the whole earth is full of his glory. And the posts of the door moved at the voice of him that cried, and the house was filled with smoke." Isaiah 6:2-4.

Isaiah, chapter six, is the only place in the Bible that explicitly mentions the seraphim. The seraphim (*fiery, burning ones*) are angelic beings associated with the prophet Isaiah's vision of God in the Temple when God called him to his prophetic ministry. Each seraph had six wings.

With one pair of wings, they hover around Jehovah's throne; and with the other two, they cover their faces and their feet,—actions symbolical of humility and adoration. The seraphim are arranged in

181

an antiphonal choir, singing the Trisagion, and their chorus is of such
volume that the sound shakes the foundations of the palace. In the
prophet's vision, they have human voices and hands (v. 6), but it cannot
be asserted with equal certainty that they possess human bodies. The
prophet leaves us in no doubt about the function of these creatures.
They are ministers of Jehovah, occupied in singing the praises of their
Sovereign, and in protecting Him from the approach of sin and evil.
The seraphim may be traced in the Imagery and symbolism of the NT
Apocalypse, where the four living creatures, in both their function and
their form, are a combination of the seraphim with the cherubim of
Ezekiel's vision. James A. Kelso.

John the Revelation, when he saw the throne room of God in
heaven, gave witness of these angelic beings around the throne,
praising God forever and ever.

> **"And the four beasts had each of them six wings**
> **about him; and they were full of eyes within: and**
> **they rest not day and night, saying, Holy, holy,**
> **holy, Lord God Almighty, which was, and is, and**
> **is to come. And when those beasts give glory and**
> **honour and thanks to him that sat on the throne,**
> **who liveth for ever and ever," Revelation 4:8-9.**

In heaven, all of God's created beings will live together in
harmony overseeing the new Jerusalem and new heaven and earth
for all of eternity.

16

Not in Heaven

"And there shall in no wise enter into it any thing that defileth, neither whatsoever worketh abomination, or maketh a lie: but they which are written in the Lamb's book of life."
Revelation 21:27.

Life in heaven with all its added beauty and the delights that are surpassing those on earth will be missing several things. The holiness of God will allow nothing evil to enter. What is missing from God's Paradise is death and the other consequences of sin.

Death invaded the reality of Adam and Eve when they sinned against God. And that rebellion has permeated all of humankind ever since. In heaven, death and dying will never again affect human life. God's judgment of Adam and Eve and their prodigy graciously limited the depths of evil that man could reach.

"He will swallow up death in victory; and the Lord GOD will wipe away tears from off all faces; and the rebuke of his people shall he take away from off all the earth: for the LORD hath spoken it." Isaiah 25:8.

We will never again have to attend a funeral service, and morticians will be out of business. God also promises to wipe away every tear from our eyes, and death shall be no more, and thus there will be no mourning, nor crying, nor pain, since old things are passed away.

In our day, we set times for mourning. We have a memorial service followed by a graveside internment service. But in Bible times, the Scripture tells of mourning periods generally lasting seven days. Someone of importance may be mourned for thirty days. This is very similar to our lowering the flag when someone famous has died. In heaven, the flags will always be at half staff.

Since Satan will be eternally incarcerated in the Lake of Fire along will all his followers and demons, there will be no more sin or anything that defiles the purity of heaven and its residents. We are headed for a glorious, deathless environment.

What we will not experience in Heaven:

"In heaven, we will have resurrection bodies with no sin nature. And we will live in a perfectly holy environment. As a natural consequence of this wondrous state of affairs, many things will be foreign to our existence in heaven. The following is just a sampling.

- *We will never have to confess a wrongdoing. With no sin in heaven, confession will unnecessary.*
- *We will never experience guilt or shame any action*

- *We will never have to repair our homes or any other items. Nothing will run down.*
- *We will never have to defend ourselves before others. Relationships will be perfect in every way.*
- *We will never have to apologize. Our actions will be focused on others instead of ourselves.*
- *We will never feel isolated or lonely. There will be a perfect expression of love between all of the redeemed.*
- *We will never have to go through rehabilitation. We remain whole and healthy for all eternity. There will never be any addicts of any kind.*
- *We will never be depressed or discouraged. We will perpetually enjoy the abundant life.*
- *We will never become tired or worn out in heaven. Our resurrection bodies will be strong and never need recuperation.*
- *There will never be offense (given or received) in heaven. All our words will be void of sin and full of grace.*
- *We will never experience envy or jealousy in heaven. Our love for others will be utterly complete and perfect, with no unwholesome emotions.*
- *We will never experience infidelity in heaven. The golden rule will unwaveringly predominate. Faithfulness will be the hallmark of heaven.*
- *We will never again lust after another person. Our hearts will be pure, with no sin whatsoever.*
- *We will never experience a misunderstanding with other people. No relationships were ever be broken.*
- *We will never have any sense of deprivation. We will never have to earn money or worry about having enough money to survive. We will have an overabundance of all we need.*
- *There will be no wars or bloodshed in heaven. The sinful attitudes that give rise to wars will be nonexistent.*

Our life in heaven will be way beyond our human understanding and even our greatest want or need. Life in heaven will be perfect.

> *"But as it is written, Eye hath not seen, nor ear heard, neither have entered into the heart of man, the things which God hath prepared for them that love him. But God hath revealed them unto us by his Spirit: for the Spirit searcheth all things, yea, the deep things of God. For what man knoweth the things of a man, save the spirit of man which is in him? Even so, the things of God knoweth no man, but the Spirit of God. Now we have received, not the spirit of the world, but the spirit which is of God; that we might know the things that are freely given to us of God. Which things also we speak, not in the words which man's wisdom teacheth, but which the Holy Ghost teacheth; comparing spiritual things with spiritual. But the natural man receiveth, not the things of the Spirit of God: for they are foolishness unto him: neither can he know them, because they are spiritually discerned. But he that is spiritual judgeth all things, yet he himself is judged of no man. For who hath known the mind of the Lord, that he may instruct him? But we have the mind of Christ." 1 Corinthians 2:9-16.*

17

Reservation for Heaven

"Jesus saith unto him, I am the way, the truth, and the life: no man cometh unto the Father, but by me. If ye had known me, ye should have known my Father also: and from henceforth ye know him, and have seen him." John 14:6-7.

"Everybody talkin' 'bout heaven ain't agoin' there:"

As this line from an old gospel song points out, not everyone is going to heaven when they die. Most people believe that once you die, everyone goes to heaven. But religions and the media do not understand how to get there. You can't go to heaven without having a reservation in the New Jerusalem recorded in the Lamb's Book of Life.

Many religions in this world believe that there is an afterlife in a place of peace and bliss. There are even three monotheistic faiths (Judaism, Christianity, Islam) that teach about a paradise after death. Most people believe that after they die, God will weigh their good works against their evil practices to determine their eternal future. Nowhere in the Bible does it show that God has a scale of judgment, nor does He grade on the curve.

Some folks place their faith in Heaven by believing if they are baptized and belong to the right church. Nowhere in the Bible does God require church membership or even baptism as a condition for his salvation.

Others believe that a loving God would send no one to Hell. They do not understand that God is Holy and that no one can approach him that is not 100% holy. To be acceptable to God based on your goodness, you would have to be perfectly sinless. It only takes a small action, a wrong thought, or selfish motive to destroy our perfect life. And most of us did that when we were little children stealing the cookies after your mother had said "no."

I know people who base their salvation on the lifetime of attending church and their parents' faith. Nowhere in the Bible does God reveal a family plan for salvation. Even being a religious person is not enough to make your reservation in heaven. Jesus explained it this way:

> *"Not every one that saith unto me, Lord, Lord, shall enter into the kingdom of heaven; but he that doeth the will of my Father which is in heaven. Many will say to me in that day, Lord, Lord, have we not prophesied in thy name? and in thy name have cast out devils? and in thy name done many wonderful works? And then will I profess unto them, I never knew you: depart from me, ye that work iniquity." Matthew 7:21-23.*

How to get a Reservation for heaven:

It is so simple to be guaranteed of Heaven that even a child can know he will spend eternity with Jesus in Heaven. Jesus told the dying thief on the cross, *"today, you will be with me in paradise."* This man had no time to do enough good works to outweigh the crimes he had committed. This man couldn't join a church or get baptized. All he could do was trust Jesus as his savior.

> *"For God so loved the world, that he gave his only begotten Son, that whosoever believeth in him should not perish, but have everlasting life. For God sent not his Son into the world to condemn the world; but that the world through him might be saved. He that believeth on him is not condemned: but he that believeth not is condemned already, because he hath not believed in the name of the only begotten Son of God. And this is the condemnation, that light is come into the world, and men loved darkness rather than light, because their deeds were evil."* John 3:16-19.

When Adam sinned, his sin-nature passed on to every human being on the earth. We all have sinned.

> *"For all have sinned, and come short of the glory of God; Being justified freely by his grace through the redemption that is in Christ Jesus: Whom God hath set forth to be a propitiation through faith in his blood, to declare his righteousness for the remission of sins that are past, through the forbearance of God; To declare, I say, at this time his righteousness: that he might be just, and*

the justifier of him which believeth in Jesus."
Romans 3:23-26.

This passage tells us we all fall short of God's acceptance, but by grace, Jesus paid as our propitiation through His shed blood on Calvary. And now God declares that we are righteous and justified through Jesus. Jesus, being the only sinless human ever, was the only one qualified to pay the price for our sins. He substituted his just life for our unjust lives.

"For the wages of sin is death (eternal separation from God)*; but the gift of God is eternal life through Jesus Christ, our Lord." Romans 6:23.*

Through faith in Jesus Christ, we receive eternal life in heaven, where He has prepared a place for us. All we need to do is believe this gospel message with the faith of a little child to receive God's eternal blessings and avoid an eternity in Satan's lake of fire.

"Then shall he say also unto them on the left hand, Depart from me, ye cursed, into everlasting fire, prepared for the devil and his angels:" Matthew 25:41.

"Where their worm dieth not, and the fire is not quenched." Mark 9:48.

"We do not suppose that a man is shooting at a target if he does not look that way; nor can we imagine that a man's ambition is fixed on heaven if he has no heavenward thoughts or aspirations. The Pilgrim turns his steps toward the place he is desirous to reach.... Till the day breaks in the shadows flee away, let us wait for the bridegroom's appearing, and the home bringing of the bride. As virgins that look forward to the marriage day let us keep our lamps trimmed, and see

to it that there is oil in our vessels, Blessed when the cry is heard, "the bridegroom cometh, any of us should be to nurse our dimly burning spark, or despairingly cry, 'our lamps are gone out' let us all be ready that we may go in through the gates into the city.

Some of you, alas! are not able to feel the joy that this subject excites in our breasts. You cannot take The Light in the throne of God and the Lamb. God grant you may. Come, now, to the throne of grace with open confession in secret contrition. It is the throne of God, who knows the nature of your sin; it the throne of the Lamb, who bore the penalty of sin, and put it away. Come to the throne of the Lamb that was slain. I entreat you to come now. So shall you find peace and reconciliation, and you shall be made meet to enter into the joy of our Lord." Charles Haddon Spurgeon.

Please don't put your eternal life in jeopardy any longer. Tell God you know you're a sinner and that you believe that Jesus died for your sins and rose again from the grave. Tell him you accept Jesus' payment of your sin penalty, and you want him to come into your life and be your Lord and master.

Just remember that God loves you enough to give the life of his only begotten son as payment for your sins.

> **"For God so loved the world, that he gave his only begotten Son (Jesus), that whosoever (enter your name) believeth in him should not perish, but have everlasting life." John 3:16.**

Ask Jesus to forgive your sins and save you now. He will become your Lord and record your reservation for heaven in the book of life. **I will meet you there.**

From The Author

Reviews are gold to an author! If you have enjoyed this book, please consider rating this book and reviewing it on Amazon.

www.amazon.com/s/ref=nb_sb_noss_
2?url=search-alias%3Daps&field-keywords=Jim+Zeigler

Thank-you

Selected Bibliography

Books:

Alcorn, Randy. *Heaven*, Tyndall House, 2004.

Barnes, Kenneth Edward. *Mystery of the Millennium*, 2016.

Eldridge, John *All Things New*, Nashville, TN. Nelson Books, 2017

Fruchtenbaum, Dr. Arnold. *The Footsteps of the Messiah*, San Antonio, TX, Ariel Ministries, 2004

Heiser, Michael. *Super Natural*. Bellingham, WA. Lexham Press, 2015.

Kennedy, D. James. *The Real Meaning of the Zodiac.* Ft Lauderdale, FL. TCRM Publishing, 2015.

Jeffery, Grant R. *Heaven: The Mystery of Angels.* Toronto, OT. Frontier Research Publications, 1996.

Liebenberg. WA. *Messianic Age—1000-Years Peace and Beyond.* Mega Restoration Store. 2017.

Mcgee, J. Vernon. *Ezekiel.* Nashville, TN. Nelson Thomas Publishers, 1991.

Otis Sr, George. *Millennium: The 1000 Year Reign of Jesus.* Simi Valley, CA. Albury Publishing, 2000.

Rhodes, Ron. *The End Times in Chronological Order.* Eugene, OR: Harvest House Publishings, 2012.

Rhodes, Ron. *What Happens After Life.* Eugene, OR: Harvest House Publishings, 2014.

Schneider, Rabbi K. A. *The Book of Revelation Revealed.* Lake Mary, FL: TCRM Publishing, 1989.

Stone, Perry. *40 Days of Teshuvah,* Cleveland, TN: Voice of Evangelism, 2006

Stone, Perry. *Secrets of the Third Heaven,* Cleveland, TN: Voice of Evangelism, 2020.

Van Impe, Jack. *Final Mysteries Unsealed.* Nashville, TN: Word Publishing, 1998.

Walvoord, John F. *Prophecy in the New Millennium.* Grand Rapids, MI: Kregel Publishing, 2001.

Internet research:

Jeremiah, David. *The Revelation Prophecy Chart* Turning Point Ministries.

www.gotquestions.org

Strongs Exhaustive Concordance of the Bible